A THOUSAND MILES IN MY SHOES

One Woman's Journey From

A Shattered Life To

An Authentic Self-Discovery

STEPHANIE C. WHITE.

Lightning Fast Book Publishing, LLC
P.O. Box 441328
Fort Washington, MD 20744

www.lfbookpublishing.com

ISBN-10: 0-9994653-1-7
ISBN-13: 978-0-9994653-1-8

TABLE OF CONTENT

DEDICATION

With love, this book is dedicated to

my mother,

Linda Evelyn White

and

my sisters,

Autumn Renee White

&

Brittany Nicole White

Preface

Your story is to be shared with the world! The lessons we learn as we endure trials, tribulations, heartbreaks, and sorrows in this life are for our benefit and the benefit of other people who find themselves in similar situations.

I wrote A Thousand Miles in My Shoes because I think it is important for everyone to know that, despite experiencing tremendous loss, they still can rise above heartbreak, pain, loneliness, and suffering. They can find hope, joy, and purpose in life and discover their authentic self. It may take time and some work; however, the search will be worthwhile.

I like to think I was placed here on this earth, at this time, for a specific reason. This reason is to help people see there is an end to their storm! Life won't always be fair; however, I believe we can live our best life if we put forth the effort.

In this book, the title of each chapter was inspired by a singer because music was and still is a tremendous part of my life. Music was a comfort to me during some of my darkest days. Today, I still enjoy music because many of the lyrics convey powerful and meaningful messages.

Acknowledgements

There is purpose in pain, and I am grateful to God for granting me the opportunity to share the purpose of my pain through the telling of my story.

I thank God for helping me put the mental puzzle pieces together to complete this project. I started this book journey in 2015, and I am very excited about how the finished product will benefit others. It wasn't easy having to relive some difficult and painful experiences, but with God's help, I was able to move forward.

I am grateful to my family for their support. Thank you, Family, for your patience. You allowed me space to shut down and shut out everything to get this done.

I especially thank you, Aunt B., for being my cheerleader throughout this whole process. Your support kept me excited every step of the way.

Thank you, Aunt Gloria, for answering my many questions and being patience with me. I know I talked your ear off at times.

Thank you, Uncle Ken, for being a fantastic listener and allowing me to quote your most famous figure of speech.

Aunt Kim, thank you for being there for me as a sister and an aunt whenever I needed to talk. Thank you for lending me your shoulder to cry on whenever I had to relive some painful situations from my past.

To my father, LT, thanks for giving me life, my love for music, and for making me dig deep. Where you were weak, I was strong. You taught me, that in life, there will be situations and how I deal with those situations is what matters most. You told me, "Either you are going to rise or you are going to fall and crumple." You also taught me the importance of forgiveness.

Thank all of you for your support. I love you, and I am blessed to have you in my life!

PROLOGUE

OUT OF BREATH

Silversun Pickups

One Unforgettable Night

"Autumn! Stephanie! Brittany! Get up and put on your coats. It's almost time to go," Linda said to her girls.

It was hard to believe fall had already arrived, and it was time to wear heavier clothing. It was a few days before Halloween, and the October nights seemed colder than usual this year. Most of the beautiful red and gold leaves had already fallen from the trees. Despite the cooler weather and the loss of the leaves, there was a festive atmosphere in the neighborhood as people had purchased pumpkins and put them in their yards and on their porches. Linda and her girls were looking forward to planning some Halloween festivities.

As the girls were putting on their coats, Linda was watching the clock on her wall. The clock was ticking closer to the time when she would have to pick up her husband, LT, from the graveyard shift at work. She had fed the children and dressed them for bed. At least, that would be one less thing she would have to do once she returned home. She even had ironed school clothes for Autumn and Stephanie to wear the next day.

Talking to herself, Linda said, "This having one car has got to end soon. I hate dragging my children out in this night air to pick up LT from work." She hated to complain because the arrangement she and her husband had really worked. She worked during the day and was able to be home at night with the kids. Of course, now after having done this for a while, it was getting old because she didn't like pulling the kids out of bed so late at night. "This will have to do for now until we can get another car," she said.

"I am tired! Why do we have to go?" Stephanie asked. "Stephanie, you know we have to go and pick your daddy up from work. Now! Please come on!" Linda said.

Linda loved her girls, but at times, Stephanie could be a handful. Outspoken and determined, she always had a question. "Mom, Brittany's birthday is in a week and she will be 2. What are we doing for her birthday?" Stephanie asked. "I have a few things planned," Linda said. "Please come on, girls. I don't want to be late picking up your dad!"

Linda secured her girls in her 1984 Cavalier. Autumn, the oldest daughter, climbed in the front passenger seat. Stephanie, the middle child and Brittany, the baby rode in the back seat. Off they went to pick up LT from work at the Jessup Correctional Institute, in Jessup, MD.

The night sky seemed darker than usual; there was not a star in sight. It was almost 11 PM. Autumn was wide- awake in the front passenger seat. Secured in her car seat, Brittany was fast asleep. Stephanie was not fully awake; she was half asleep.

As she drove along the highway, who knows what this young mother was thinking? Maybe, she was thinking about her family on the Eastern Shore, her career as a Correctional Officer, and her 30th birthday which was soon to come in two years. Perhaps, she was thinking how well she was doing in life. She had three adorable girls, her husband, a career, a home, a good family, and her health. What more could a woman ask for!!

One thing for sure, Linda was eager to pick up her husband from work and get her daughters back home and put them to bed.

Then, it happened! Out of nowhere! Bright lights flashed in Linda's eyes. "Where is this fool going?" she yelled. The dark pick-up truck seemed to be in the other lane, but why was he coming towards her and her girls?

PLEASE STOP! IT'S TOO LATE! SOMEONE HAD CROSSED THREE LANES OF TRAFFIC! THERE WAS AN UNGODLY SOUND OF METAL UPON METAL! A HORRIFIC COLLISON! FLASHING LIGHTS & SIRENS EVERYWHERE ….

1

PLEASE DON'T GO

Immature

Those Left Behind

The accident occurred on Wednesday evening, October 28, 1987, in Howard County, Maryland. My mother, Linda and my sisters, Autumn and Brittany, and I never arrived at the Jessup Correctional Institute to pick up my father from work. Life can throw you some real curves at times, however, no one was expecting this!

When this horrific accident occurred, I was 5. Due to the impact of the car crash, I was flown to the University of Maryland Shock Trauma Unit, in Baltimore, MD. One of my legs was broken, and I had suffered a concussion. I was put in body cast which started right above my navel and extended all the way down my right leg which was suspended in the air by a sling. Two surgical pins supported the cast.

In the next room at the hospital, Brittany was in a coma. My baby sister, who was a week shy of her second birthday, was neither moving nor speaking. Her head and face were covered in cuts. In time, she would have permanent scars. Brittany suffered from severe head trauma that caused severe brain damage. Trauma to both of her legs later stunted her growth.

Due to the injuries, she sustained in the accident, my oldest sister, Autumn, who was 7, died on her way to the hospital. My mother, Linda, who was 28, was killed instantly due to the impact of the head-on crash. It was later determined she and Autumn had died within five minutes of each other.

Someone might say that two deaths occurred that day. Yet, I see the occurrence of many deaths in the form of hopes, dreams, and companionship. Not only did my oldest sister and mother die, but the security and quality of life Brittany and I had with our father died. So much would change for both sides of my family.

Who was this man who caused such a tragic mess? Why did he do it? Why was he drinking and driving? Why did this man not realize he was crossing three traffic lanes and heading in the wrong direction?

The driver who caused the accident was 38 years old. A day before the accident, his license had been renewed after having been suspended for two months due to driving drunk.

Ironically, because of his injuries, he was taken to the same hospital where my mother, my sisters, and I were taken.

After his release from the hospital, it was reported by the news media that he tried to commit suicide because of the deaths he had caused. When he went to court, he was charged with two counts of manslaughter, convicted of speeding, reckless driving, driving while intoxicated and failing to drive on the right side of the road. He received five years in prison for the crime and six years of probation. Did the punishment fit the crime? What's the price of taking the lives of two people?

When my family learned of the accident, they were devastated! We had been living in Baltimore County for about six months and just that quick, the pages of our lives turned from good to bad. I don't think my family had ever known a tragedy such as this one!

What should have been a regular night at work turned into a nightmare for my father. When my mother didn't arrive on time to pick him up from work, my father asked a co-worker to give him a ride home. On the way home, he and his co-worker came upon the accident scene. Can you imagine the thoughts that were going through my father's mind when he saw our car, the ambulances, and many police cars? I can imagine my father felt a pain like no other pain, a pain that made him sick, a pain that could never be healed! In the blink of an eye, my father's life changed forever. He went from being a married man to a widower and sadly, he suffered the loss of his oldest child.

The Loss of a Loved One

Have you ever lost someone close to you? How did you feel? Were you angry? Were you frustrated? Did you feel numb? Did you have questions? Well, I had many questions. I had questions no one could answer! Why did my sister, Autumn, have to die so young? What purpose did this serve? At such a young age, did my sister already carry out her purpose here on earth? How is that possible? I asked myself all these questions. Doesn't one have to live a long life to carry out their purpose in this life? Does the length of someone's life have nothing to do with the purpose God has for one's life? I know if my sister could have had a choice, she would still want to be here. I felt cheated. I was confused and hurt.

I often look at my life and wonder what it would have been like to have had my older sister by my side. We missed out on talks, arguments, sharing secrets, first school dances, boyfriends, high school graduations, college graduations, weddings, etc. My sister will never get to experience these things. As I got older, I had to accept the fact that God's plans are not my plans. Though I would have loved to have had my older sister here with me to share in these life experiences, I have had to realize that God had other plans for Autumn.

A Flower

A beautiful flower! This is how I describe my mother! When I talk to people who knew my mother, they have nothing but wonderful things to say about her. My mother was a beautiful woman who had a great heart and a beautiful soul. People tell me that I look a lot like my mother.

My mother loved her girls, and she had her whole life ahead of her. She had begun working at the Jessup Correctional Institute, and I believe my mother was happy and excited about being able to build a life she wanted for her family. She was building a career she wanted as well.

Twenty-eight years old is such a young age to pass away. It is funny how, up until I was 28, I felt as if I could relate to my mother. I would ask myself, "What would my mother do in this situation? How would my mother act in this situation? How would she feel in this situation?" I would try to center myself and literally try to feel what my mother either would feel, think or say in a situation. This allowed me to feel close to my her.

Sadly, on my 29th birthday, I felt lost. Because my mother died at the age of 28, I felt as if I could no longer relate to her. At my new age, I tried to think of what my mother would say, do or think. I drew a blank! I felt cheated!

I missed so many things: not having my mother walk me to class on my first day of school in the second grade; hugs and kisses I surely needed from her; the talks about boys, sex, etc.; sharing my thoughts about my likes and my dislikes; celebrating her on Mother's Day and on her birthday; and sharing my high school, undergraduate and graduate school celebrations.

My mother will never get to see my new home. She never will get the opportunity to know the success of my business and to meet some of the people who have encouraged me throughout the years. These are people who have sown into my life and have helped me on this journey. I call them friends; however, they are like family.

My mother will never get to dance at my wedding! This is generally a time in a woman's life where she needs her mother, and my mother's seat will be empty. Life is crazy! At times, it's been very difficult to accept the cards I have been dealt.

A Husband's Pain

I can only imagine what my dad felt after my mother's passing. He lost his wife, his friend, his soul mate, and his confidant. A thousand thoughts must to have run through my father's head: memories of their dates, their wedding, family outings, things he said and things he didn't get a chance to say, and events he wished he could correct.

My father thought he had more time. Life has a way of showing you signs and a lot of times, we don't notice the signs until after something has happened. One must be spiritually in tune to notice these signs. Sometimes, we ignore the signs we are shown. What I have learned through this journey is everything is connected.

When I sit and think sometimes, I think about all the things I missed out on not having my family unit together. I think about the man who was the cause of this accident. Where is he today? Does he know what damage he has done? In a conversation with my aunts, I learned the man who caused this tragedy in my family is still living and has tried to take his own life on more than one occasion. My compassion for people makes me feel sorry for him. I am a spiritual being and though I am deeply hurt by the loss of my mother and my sister, I do not and would never want the man who caused such a mess of my life to take his own life.

Memories of what used to be and thoughts of what could have been often flood my mind. On this day, in this life, at this moment, how did I, Stephanie White, get to where I was before and where I am today? There clearly is more to my story, my life, my truth, and my family

2

JOURNEY TO THE PAST

Aaliyah

The Beginning

LT and Linda married on September 4, 1978, at Centennial United Methodist Church, in Fairmount, Maryland. It was a lavish affair fit for a Royal Court! The bride wore white and the groom wore baby blue. Linda had just graduated high school a year earlier, and LT had joined the Army and was scheduled for Basic Training, in Georgia, in November. The couple was excited about starting their lives together!

For more than six years, while in the army, LT, was stationed in the United States and overseas. In 1980, LT and Linda decided to start a family and they welcomed their first child, Autumn. Two years later, I was born. Both LT and Linda felt their family wasn't quite complete and in 1985, they welcomed their third child, Brittany. Our family became known as THE FANTASTIC 5! Lt, Linda, Autumn, Brittany and me.

Life with my family was good. There were times of laughter, fun, and plenty of love! I remember being surrounded by many relatives from both my mother's and father's side of the family.

For a while, my sisters, my parents, and I lived with my grandparents in Fairmount. During this time, I developed quite a bond with my oldest sister as we played together. Our sister Brittany was only a baby, so the amount of time we spent playing with her was limited.

Before I began attending school for a half day, I fondly remember watching television with my grandparents. From Monday through

Friday, we watched the noonday news and the CBS soap operas: **The Young & The Restless, The Bold & The Beautiful, As The World Turns** and **The Guiding Light. The Oprah Winfrey Show** at 4 PM was the last program we watched before Grandma started preparing dinner. Once I began school, I surely did miss those soap operas!

Living in the country was a great experience. I loved the gravel and dirt roads which led to some of the most beautiful homes in the countryside. My grandmother lived in a two-story, light green home which was up a dirt road we called a lane. There was so much nature to be seen at her home. Fruit trees, grape vines, and flowers grew in abundance.

Not only did I see a lot of nature, I also saw a lot of dogs. I am not sure how it happened, but of my parents' three children, I was the one who was terrified of DOGS, and there were many dogs in Fairmount. Getting on and off the bus for school each day was horrifying for me because the lady down the lane, in the house by my bus stop, had dogs. Today, I laugh with my relatives about those times. A girl had to be saved on several occasions from dogs in those days!

It's not easy having to rear three kids; however, having one of those kids refuse to eat makes the job more difficult. I was the kid who would not eat! Maybe, I simply wasn't hungry. Usually, my mother would make me sit at the table until I had eaten everything on my plate. Sometimes, sleep would overtake me before I accomplished what she wanted me to do. It was a while before my metabolism began to function. and I wouldn't stop eating! Hmmm! Now, I wish for those days!

The Family Move

When you are a child, you don't ever know everything adults know. You will not know or realize when things are bad or when things are good! I know my family did a really good job of keeping children out of "grown folks business" because as a child, I had no idea my family didn't have a lot of money. They had a lot of love, but not a lot of money!

In 1987, right after my fifth birthday on August 28, my dad moved our family to Baltimore, MD. He arrived before we arrived and begin a new job as a Correctional Officer at the Jessup Correctional Institute.

At the same time, one of my mother's sisters and her family moved to Baltimore and lived in a house across the street from us. My mother's brother lived close to us as well. Again, I was surrounded by family.

Life seemed good in 1987! My father rented a duplex for our family, and Autumn and I met some new friends when we enrolled in Beechfield Elementary School.

I remember my family didn't have much; however, my sister and I had comfortable beds made on the floor and a dresser for our clothes. We had a couch, a television in the living room, a kitchen table and chairs. We had some toys, but mostly we had each other.

My dad played outside with us girls, and my mother took us for walks in the park. Our other relatives who lived nearby often accompanied us

My sisters and I enjoyed spending time together watching shows such as **Give Me a Break**, starring Nell Carter; Star Search, hosted by Ed McMahon; **Elf**, and **Jem & The Holograms.**

Life was good, but little did I know that things were about to change in the worst way. Two months after my birthday, on October 28, my mother and Autumn were killed in that horrible car crash I earlier described to you.

3

GET BY

Talib Kweli

Picking Up the Pieces

A month after the accident, I was released from the hospital. For about a year, I lived with one of my mother's sisters, on the Eastern Shore of Maryland.

Due to the full body cast I wore to promote the healing of my broken leg, I was reduced to lying flat in a hospital bed at my Aunt's house for what seemed liked forever! I couldn't turn left or right, due to the heaviness of the cast. When I needed to relieve myself, I had to use a bed pan.

Even in my terrible condition, I have fond memories of watching cartoons and other shows during my stay at my aunt's house. **Mr. Roger's Neighborhood** was one of my favorite shows.

After the accident, I couldn't remember much of what happened that night. I remember being very sleepy that evening and drifting in and out of sleep while in the back seat.

One day, I asked my aunt how did I find out my mother and sister had passed away? She said to me that while I was in the hospital, I kept asking for my mother and when was she was coming to get me. I was told that my mother was not going to be able to come to get me because she had passed away in the car accident. I really didn't know what those words meant. What do you mean my mother is not coming for me?

My aunt said that I had a look of confusion on my face. How could a 5-year-old comprehend the fact that her mother died and was never going to come and get her? I only got to spend five years with the woman who birthed me. I think I wore that same confused look on my face for years after the accident.

I would often have out-of-body experiences wherein I couldn't believe that this life that I was living was really happening to me. I would say "This can't be possible!" Then, when I would take another look around at myself and my life, I had to face reality.

In November 1987, Brittany, my baby sister, spent the beginning of her second year of life in the hospital. For three months, she was in a coma. Finally, in January 1988, she opened her eyes.

Brittany had regressed to the stage of a newborn baby. Because of all the damage to her brain, her beautiful hair had to be cut very low for the doctors to gain access to her skull. My sister never regained the ability to speak and learn like others. She would have the mind of a 2-year-old for the rest of her life! Because of the injuries to her legs, Brittany would forever walk with a limp,

After Brittany emerged from the comma, she had a long road to recovery. She spent months at The Kennedy Krieger Institute for Handicapped Children, in Baltimore, MD, where her team of doctors were some of the best! I am grateful to them for the outstanding care they provided for my sister.

During Brittany's lifetime, some people referred to her as being retarded. This statement made me feel sad. The word, retarded, had such a negative vibe. Whenever I heard the insensitive comment, I would explain my sister's disability and the circumstances which created her condition. "She has special needs; however, she is not retarded," was my response to their remarks.

Eventually Brittany came back to the Eastern Shore of MD and was transferred to the Holly Center, in Salisbury, where she continued her therapy and rehabilitation.

A few months after Brittany came back to the Eastern Shore, my full body cast was removed. My leg had healed, and it was time to head to physical therapy. Because I had sat so long in the full body cast, I had lost my full ability to walk and had to learn to walk again. My bones and muscles weren't strong enough anymore, and I needed therapy to regain the use of my muscles. At first, I simply sat because I couldn't remember how to just get up and walk. Then, when I tried to stand, I would fall. I went to physical therapy for months. It would take months to undo what the car accident had done.

My dad, on the other hand, was trying to figure out how to move forward with two broken-hearted daughters who would never be the same.

Life had taken on a new meaning. It didn't seem too kind anymore. The smile I once had was gone; the security I once knew in life was gone; and life just wasn't the same. I wish I could turn back the clock. I wish we all could wake up again on that Wednesday morning, October 28, 1987, and everything would be different.

During my alone time, I often asked God a series of questions: Why was my life spared? What sense did it make to take our mother and older sister and leave Brittany and me alone with our father to fend for ourselves. Girls need their mother! Life can be so unfair.

Eventually, Brittany and I returned to live with my father, LT, in a two-story townhouse in Salisbury, MD. Both Brittany and I had our own room. Our new home had three bedrooms, two bathrooms, a combined living room and dining room, and a kitchen.

Two years passed. I was 7 and Brittany was 4. She was doing much better and was able to walk. At times, she still used a wheel chair. Most of the time, my dad picked her up and carried her whenever we went somewhere.

I was in the second grade and attended Prince Street Elementary School. The wonderful thing about this school was that Brittany, despite her disability, was eligible to attend the same school. Brittany rode the bus and, I walked to school with a friend.

Although the accident had occurred two years ago, my dad, Brittany, and I still were trying to find a new rhythm to this thing called life. My dad was working at the Eastern Shore Correctional Institute in Princess Anne, MD, and he either found a relative or a babysitter to care for us when he wasn't at home. Instead of **The Fantastic 5**, we were now **The Three Musketeers.**

To the outside world, our lives appeared normal. The reality was our lives were anything but normal. There was so much pain! My dad tried to dull his pain, including the use of abusive substances and the purchase of cars, furniture, and other material things. For a moment, it seemed to work, and then the pain that hadn't been dealt with returned and the process of trying to numb the pain would be repeated.

In the second grade, I spent a lot of time outside in the hallway at school because I had disrupted the class by being the class clown. Eventually, the teacher moved my desk right beside her desk where she could keep a closer watch on me. I look back on those days in my young life and conclude that my reasons for acting out in class were because I wanted attention from my father who was sometimes pre-occupied. Oftentimes, I felt as if he didn't care.

One day, my father came to school for me. I can't remember if my dad had to come to my school because of my behavior or because he was just observing my class. Regardless of the reason, I was extremely excited that my dad came to my school! I know it sounds silly, but I was overjoyed because my dad had come to see about me. It made me feel wanted; it made me feel good; and it made me feel like the other kids who had parents who cared. I was starving for attention.

I look back on that day and though I was excited, it was also very sad. What that moment showed me was I was lacking some things in my life a child should have had.

I was a very smart child; however, I did not utilize the smarts God gave me. Because I craved the attention of my father, I neglected attention to my studies. I failed all subjects during my second year of school. I received all E's and had to repeat the grade.

Whenever I received my report card, my dad was pre-occupied and didn't pay attention to my grades. I capitalized on this by showing him things when he was busy. It only hurt me in the long run because having to repeat the second grade was no fun.

My Sister's Keeper

As my dad, sister and I continued to move forward, we found a new rhythm in life. I guess we really had no choice, but to find a new way to live.

To make clothes shopping easier, my dad purchased identical outfits for Brittany and me. With three years difference in our ages, Brittany and I clearly were not twins. I guess it was easier for my dad to buy two of an item as opposed to shopping for two different items.

My dad had three toy-like rubber California Raisins. They represented music, food, and water. Each of the Raisins symbolized each one of us and what we loved! My dad loved food; I loved music; and Brittany loved water! She would stay in the water all day if you allowed her.

The bond between Brittany and me was very strong. She had a way of knowing when something was wrong or when I was upset. When I cried, she cried. It was like we were twin souls! She seemed to have known what I was feeling, and I knew what she was feeling. Brittany and I had some of the same mannerisms and sometimes Brittany would mirror some of the same things I did.

Brittany was a special child. Despite her brain damage, she had the ability to hum the tune of a song after she heard it only once. Truly, this was God's gift to her.

Brittany loved toys which made sounds. One of her favorite toys was a little piano which played music when she tapped on the keys. Oftentimes, she would try to sing along with the music. Just as she tried to sing, she tried to talk. Every now and then, she was able to say her name. Most of the time, the damaged area of her brain did not permit this to happen. This, however, did not stop her from trying. My sister was a remarkable and smart child!

Brittany really had something special about her which I believe a lot of people couldn't see because they couldn't see beyond her disability. I think some people missed out on knowing the true essence of my sister.

Childhood Heartbreak

My dad was born on June 16, 1956, and he comes from a huge family which includes twenty siblings. People who know my dad describe him as having "swag," a stylish confidence that might be a plus or a negative, depending on how you view it.

As a young man, Dad loved to sing. He was a sharp dresser, and the ladies loved him. Of course, he loved the ladies as well!

My dad is far from perfect and like all of us, he made some mistakes in his life. Some of the mistakes are ones I will never understand. On the other hand, there are mistakes he made which I do understand.

I believe, when my mother and sister died, my dad was not able to process what happened. Sometimes, he seemed to be in a mental fog. Because I craved his attention, I couldn't relate to his behavior.

When my dad started dating again, I made a statement which was the worst thing I could have ever said. I told my dad's girlfriend that I wished my dad had died instead of my mother. My father heard about this statement I made, and he was hurt by it. I regret saying those words, and I regret him hearing what I said. At the time, I really missed my mother and I was probably mad with my dad!

My dad had a lot of friends! Everyone knew LT. At times, these friendships irritated me to no end because they interfered with the time Brittany and I could have spent with our father.

As a child, I remember going to some of the homes of my dad's friends. My sister and I stayed in the car while my dad was inside of the houses. We played with our toys in the car and waited for our dad. At the time, I didn't know our toys were used to occupy us while my dad spent what seemed like hours with his friends. Now, there were a few times when I became impatient with my dad. If I thought Brittany and I were outside in the car just a little longer than what we needed to be, I would blow the car horn to get my father's attention. Eventually, he would come out of the house and we would go home.

What was he thinking? Maybe, he wasn't thinking at all. Who were these friends of his? Why did they think his behavior was okay? Maybe, they had no idea his kids were waiting in the car for him.

Even as a youngster, I was nosey! I always had my eyes and my ears open! I saw things I probably should not had seen.

Sometimes, my father would have parties at our house. Some of his friends would come and stay for hours. There were substances used which should never have been present in an environment where children lived.

Sometimes we were in the dark upstairs; we didn't have light in our bedroom. I'm not sure why that was the case! Weird and Interesting! Sometimes during these parties, Brittany and I would go to bed hungry. How do you forget about your kids upstairs and forget to feed them? Who does this?

One night, my dad did come upstairs after his party was over and attempt to feed us dinner. It was very late, and I was sleepy. There was no dinner for me that night.

I look back on these moments and they make me sad because I would never treat a child like this. I guess my father didn't realize what he was doing. God had to have been watching over Brittany and me because anything could have happened to us during the times my father was not as attentive as he should have been. We could have been robbed, killed, or kidnapped. For sure, God sent His angels to protect us!

Everything wasn't always doom and gloom. I remember a very happy moment when one of my dad's girlfriend came to our townhouse and decorated my bedroom. This really brought some joy to my life. Reminiscing about that day, I smile because I had prayed to God a lot during those days, asking Him to bring Brittany and me a female role model who would come and stay with us. Don't get me wrong. I loved my dad; however, we girls needed a woman in our lives. I remember praying as hard as I could pray. I was not sure if God heard me, but I prayed anyway.

While a babysitter was watching us one night, she told me that she heard a noise. It sounded as if someone was going up the stairs. She told me that she believed it was my mother, coming to check on her girls. I believed it was my mother as well. My mother had not forgotten about her girls, left here on this earth! She and Autumn were now our Angels and they kept us safe! They had to be the ones watching over us.

Soon our babysitter became our dad's new girlfriend, and we moved from Salisbury to my dad's girlfriend's house in Princess Anne, MD.

I was 8 and attended Princess Anne Elementary School. I was in second grade for the second time and remembered the failing grades I received during the last school year? Well not anymore! This time I understood what I had to do! I paid more attention in school and to my grades! I almost had straight A's this time! I was passing with flying colors!

My dad's girlfriend had children of her own. Some were older, and some were younger than Brittany and me.

It was interesting being in someone else's space. I learned the meaning of "hand-me-downs" very quickly.

As a child, all I could do was go along with the living arrangement in which I found myself. I had no power to change anything.

My dad's girlfriend had a small dog, and I was not a friend of dogs! In fact, there were a few dogs in the community where we lived. One day, after seeing one of the dogs, I climbed onto the top of a car and sat there for most of the day. I think I even used the bathroom up there that day. For the life of me, I have no idea how I eventually made it down off the car and into the house that evening.

One thing this house had was something I was not used to seeing. It had roaches! Oh my! You think I am terrified of dogs, you haven't seen anything yet! I hate things that crawl! I hate bugs! I hate bugs! I hate bugs! Even today as an adult, I hate bugs and I am terrified of them! I can't say I ever got used to them at my dad's girlfriend's house. Who can? They were everywhere!

The house would get "bombed" to get rid of the insects. Sometimes it worked, and sometimes it didn't. This was an issue for several years until we moved to another house.

Now don't get me wrong. We had some fun times, we really did. We laughed, joked, played, listened to music, and had a good time. I was even introduced to Rap music and Rap artists such as Dr. Dre, Snoop Dog, and Eazy-E. One of my favorite songs at the time was by Dr. Dre!

Eventually we moved to an apartment house in Princess Anne. I was about 9 and had met my best friend, Pam. We were inseparable in school. Life was great! We lived in the same neighborhood, and we went to school together.

There were so many kids in our neighborhood. We would have neighborhood kick ball games and play hide and seek. Oh! To be a kid again!

During this time, I was getting my hair straightened, looking at boys, and going to summer camp. Oh yes, I started my period! I guess I was officially a woman at the age of 9! I was horrified when I started my period at such a young age! Try going to summer camp with a sanitary napkin in your bag! It was the worst! Nevertheless, I kept it moving.

By now, Brittany was advancing more. She was saying more words, she was singing a lot, and walking much better. Her use of the wheel chair had decreased. When Brittany was happy, I was happy.

She received more attention from my father than I did. I knew it was because she required more attention than I did, but that didn't stop me from feeling a little jealous. There were a few times I allowed my jealously to get the best of me. You best believe that only happened once or twice because my little sister meant the world to me.

I hate to admit it, but there was one time I became embarrassed while pushing my sister in her wheel chair. We were going for a walk, and I saw a boy whom I liked. He spoke to us. Then, he kept staring at Brittany. I guess he was looking at her wheel chair. I didn't feel so good. This was the first time I had been out in the neighborhood with Brittany and had run into someone from school. Other than Pam, my best friend, no one at school knew anything about my life outside of school. When I came to my senses, I reminded myself that Brittany was my sister who had a disability. End of discussion!

Prior to my graduation from elementary school, we moved to a single-family house next door to the apartment in which we had been living, and it had a large yard. My dad started growing fruits and vegetables. He enjoyed this work, and his garden became his pride and joy!

After living in that house for a while, we moved to another single-family home which was much smaller.

In the process of all the moving, I got two new little sisters. The once babysitter, turned girlfriend, was the mother of my two little sisters whom I love dearly. Now, my dad was the father of not only three girls, but five girls!

Life was relatively alright; however, I wasn't completely happy. My 10-year-old self planned to run away. I packed my bags, and my destination was my aunt's house which was right across the highway; this was the same aunt that I lived with when I got out of the hospital, right after the car accident. That plan did not materialize. I got a beating, and no one went any place!

I went through several other changes during these times. I started calling my dad's girlfriend, Mother. I knew she wasn't my mother, but I wanted to feel connected to her other children who called her Mom, so I asked her if I could call her Mother, and she told me that I could.

4

EVERYBODY HURTS

R.E.M.

Little Girl Lost

One night, when I was about 9 or 10, a phrase popped in my head. I planned to say it in school the next day. Now, I had no idea what this phrase meant, but I was determined to say it anyway. I had no idea what the response would be from the people at school, and I had no idea why the thought popped in my head. So, the next day came and just like I said I would do, I said it! While in the hallway, I blurted out to one of my teachers, "I am going to commit suicide." My teacher took my comment seriously and immediately contacted the school counselor. What was very interesting is that I think I was smiling when I said it! I cringe now thinking about that day. What was I thinking?   I met with the counselor. She asked me if I knew what I was saying. I told her that I did not know. Looking back, I guess my behavior was another attempt to get attention from whomever would give it to me. The counselor never told my father what happened that day.

During this time in my life, because I had grown older, I was more responsible for helping to care for Brittany. Because of her brain damage, she could neither tell you when she was hungry nor tell you when she needed to use the bathroom. So, one morning, I was getting my sister ready for school and noticed she didn't have any clean underpants. Having no idea about what to do, I didn't change her underpants. She left for school in soiled underwear.

All day at school, I thought about what had happened that morning. I knew if my dad learned about the matter, he would be upset. But, what was I to do? I was a child who didn't know what decision to make. I had a healthy fear of my father. At times, he would raise his voice and sometimes, I got a beating.

Not knowing what to do, I went to school that day and told my counselor that I was nervous about going home. Of course, the counselor called my father.

When I got home from school, I got a beating because I had told what went on at home that morning. In Black families, one thing you do not do is tell the family's business. That was the last beating I received with the belt!! Thank God for that because my dad was heavy-handed!

Who is Stephanie White?

Who is Stephanie? To understand who I am now, you would have to first understand who I was as a youngster. Pink dress, ponytail, black and white shoes! This is what I wore on picture day, in 1986, when I was in kindergarten. I had just celebrated my fourth birthday that August, and my mother made sure I looked like a girl. Inside of me was a spirit that wanted to be FREE! FREE to run, jump and climb trees! A spirit that wanted to leap off steps and into the sky, if I could. Though dresses were cute, I wanted to wear pants and pants only!

Being the middle child wasn't always easy. I didn't get as much attention as the baby of the family and as the oldest child. I was stuck in the middle! Based on the stories I have been told, I had my own way of distinguishing myself from my sisters.

I think I always had a tomboy hiding inside of me. For a long time as a child, I was very skinny and athletic. I loved to perform splits. I was something to see!

Along with my flexibility, I had a knack for climbing trees even if I were wearing a skirt. One day, a branch from the tree tore my skirt. To make matters worse, I did a split and damaged the skirt even more! I was very nervous about going home that day. What girl climbs a tree in a dress, does a split, and then tries to hide it by walking backwards? Of course, it didn't help the situation. Eventually, I had to tell what happened to my skirt. Even though I was a girl, that didn't stop me from doing what boys did. I was a tomboy! What can I say!

As I continued to get older, my love for wearing pants grew more and more. Wearing dresses meant I had to watch how I sat. I had to act like a lady! FREEDOM was what I wanted!

When I became a teenager, something began to happen to me. I started watching what other teenagers were wearing, and I wanted to be like the kids at school. I wanted to wear my hair differently and carry a certain purse, etc. I wanted to fit in with my peers. I am not quite sure when it started; however, at some point in my teenage years, I began to copy other people's styles instead of developing my own style.

By the time I was in high school, I had completely let go of the struggle to be my own individual self. I had decided it was much easier to follow the crowd. What this meant was denial of my true self and my true fashion. When you constantly move from house to house and there are so many changes in your life, you can only hold onto who you are for so long and then, you get lost. At least, that's how it was for me. I was trying to identify with something or someone! Who I was went right out the door and my life became about fitting in with other people.

5

COMFORTER

Shai

Comfort for My Thoughts

In my world, I felt lost. As a child, I didn't know where to turn for comfort. As a young lady, I turned to music as my comforter: Midnight Star, Sade, Babyface, Luther Vandross, Whitney Houston, Jodeci, Deborah Cox, Janet Jackson, Anita Baker, Roberta Flack, Brian McKnight, Karyn White, Betty Wright, Missy Elliott, Timbaland & Magoo, Faith Evans, Biggie Smalls, AeroSmith, the David Matthew's Band, and so many other great artists helped me sort through my feelings.

Music can be a healer, a soul-soother, a distractor, and a memory-maker. It has a way of stamping a moment in time in one's life!

My love for music probably started when I was in my mother's womb because my father loved to sing. I'm sure he sang to my mother when she was pregnant with me. At one time, my dad sang with a group who performed in the night clubs. He loved the popular singers of his day: Michael Jackson, The Temptations, The Mandrills, Smokey Robinson, Harold Melvin and the Blue Notes, and other artists.

Dad said that Freddie Jackson's hit song, "You Are My Lady" was his and my mother's song. Every time I hear this song, it makes me think of better times when my mother and my father were together. I shed a few tears when I think of what could have been for our family if not for that terrible day in October 1987.

Music has been a part of my family's life for years! No! I don't have any famous musical artists in my family; however, I do have an aunt who once recorded a song in a studio! She never won a Grammy, but her experience is worth mentioning.

In my family, both my maternal and paternal aunts sing in church choirs. If I say so myself, they sing quite well.

In high school, four of my cousins and I formed The Voices of Praise, a Gospel group. We mostly sang for local events, and it was fun while it lasted.

I AM MUSIC!

When I hear "I Am Music" by Timbaland & Magoo, featuring Aaliyah, I think of who I am. I AM MUSIC!

Classical, Jazz, R & B, Old School Rap, Rock, Pop, Gospel, Instrumental, Disco, Neo-Soul - you name it and Stephanie loves it!

My own personal love affair with music started in the 80's, the year was 1989 to be exact. I was a little 7-year-old girl who wore blue-stone washed jeans, pigtails in my hair, an old-school baseball shirt, and high-top sneakers.

At this time in my life, I was a huge Michael Jackson fan and I had his "I'm Bad" cassette tape. I remember wearing out this album in my boom box and Walk-Man player. Both my father and I loved this album and would discuss the music. That brought us closer together and even now, music brings us closer.

Over the years, music continued to do for me what no human could do! Music was a comforter to me in times of worry and sorrow. Music was there to sooth my soul and my sprit when I was wounded! Music saved me at a young age during a time when I didn't know I needed saving. Music was my distraction from times when I was hungry, and there was no food to eat.

Music served me well when I wanted to daydream. It made me feel better about my life, and things seemed to instantly change for me. I would begin to daydream of a life filled with happiness, friends, and adventures. I dreamed of an ideal family life. Music helped me create a fantasy life I hoped to live one day.

My daydreams would take me on adventures of hiking with friends near deserts and waterfalls or adventures of living in a household where I had all my sisters and both of my parents.

Music was therapeutic for me. Often after listening to music, I would be in a state of happiness. A once sad child, would now have a smile on her face. Some would have called it crazy, but I called it survival.

Self-made Coping Mechanism

There are certain secrets I figured I would take to the grave with me. Then, there are secrets people found out about me and I didn't really care.

As a youngster, I begin to use rocking as a coping mechanism. Backward and forward! Backward and forward! It didn't matter whether I was standing, sitting, or lying in bed, I had mastered this technique of rocking. I would rock backward, forward, and side to side.

I don't even remember how it all got started. I believe it started right after my mother died. When I was a little girl, I would cry for my mother and rock myself to sleep! That's my earliest memory of using this rocking technique. When I was younger, the rocking mostly involved crying and as I got older, the rocking technique took on a whole new meaning! The rocking was now coupled with listening to music, which was already therapeutic for me! Then, came the daydreaming. I always wanted my life to be something different than what it was, so daydreaming helped me cope with my present life. I know this sounds crazy to some, but this was how I survived growing up! I drifted off to another land through my daydreams. I could be anyone I wanted to be. I either could be the cute girl next door or the Super woman who came to SAVE THE DAY!

I often felt embarrassed about this rocking, but for the most part it didn't bother me too much because it was what I felt I needed at the time. For years, I continued this coping mechanism. My family knew about it, but they didn't shame me about it. When I became an adult, I was often reminded of those times. My family and I would laugh about it.

6

REUNITED & IT FEELS SO GOOD

Peaches & Herb

The Love of Grandparents

Life was complicated enough without my mother. Then, for some unknown reason, my father would not allow my mother's mom and step-father to see Brittany and me. I don't know what he had against them. Whatever it was, it didn't have anything to do with us or at least it shouldn't have. We needed our grandparents in our life, and it finally happened one Sunday morning when I was attending church with my dad's girlfriend's family. I saw my grandmother in the choir box. She was telling the church that she hadn't seen Brittany and me since our mother died more than four years ago and she missed us. My grandmother was sad! Little did she know, I was right in the audience that Sunday. When the service was over, I went over to my grandmother and gave her the BIGGEST HUG! We were reunited that day, and life was never the same!

This was a very happy day in my life. I never knew how much I missed my grandparents until that day. Having Grandma and Pop-pop back in my life helped me find stability in a world that was constantly changing. From that moment forward, my sister Brittany and I would spend lots of time with our grandparents in Fairmount.

Grandma was a tall, gentle lady with skin the color of caramel. She had eight children. Pop-Pop was a tall man who loved biscuits with syrup, and he loved to sing.

My grandparents' home was the meeting place. Whenever Brittany and I went to visit, there always were other people coming to see my grandparents.

I have fond memories of being in the country in the summertime and watching Grandma sterilize Mason jars and their lids in large pots of boiling water as she prepared to can peaches and make fresh preserves. She had a grape vine in the backyard and an apple tree as well.

I enjoyed watching Grandma pick crabs with one of her friends. They put the crabmeat in containers to be sold.

Grandma believed in homemade food. She cooked the best meals. My favorite was her spaghetti! Grandma baked fresh bread and cooked neck bones and potatoes. You name it! She cooked it!

I have so many fond memories of being with her. I remember the summer mornings when she would wash clothes and hang them outside on the line to dry. Then, there were times when I would play house in Grandma's clothes. She lived in the country and up a dirt lane, so no one was outside or around to see me.

Grandma always said that she would never beat her grandchildren because they got enough beatings at home! Grandma was true to her word. She never hit us.

Watching television with Grandma brought back memories of when my family lived with her and Pop-pop just before the accident occurred. I can still remember Grandma, Pop-pop, Brittany, and me watching **The Color Purple** for the first time on television. Of course, it was on VHS!

Pop-pop always fixed my breakfast! He used a cast-iron frying pan to cook me the best scrapple and eggs. Although he knew what

I wanted every day, he would jokingly ask me what I wanted. He always knew it was going to be scrapple and eggs!

My grandfather would get me anything I wanted, and I always wanted candy: Snickers, Kit Kat bars, and Butterfingers. He would go to Genos, the corner store in Fairmount, where people could play their numbers and get the best cheese burgers! Pop-pop spoiled me! I am grateful for the love he showed me when I needed it the most!

Sunday mornings at my grandparents' house sounded like Sunday! Early in the morning, Grandma turned on the record player and gospel music could be heard throughout the house. After a hearty breakfast, we went to Centennial United Methodist Church, in Upper Fairmount. This was the church Grandma had attended since she was a child. Sometimes, we stayed in church all day. If it were Easter Sunday, we could count on being at church for at least four hours for Sunday morning service! Grandma was the church treasurer, so we sometimes attended meetings with her during the week.

Sometimes, my dad would come and pick us up from Grandma and Pop-pop's house. Other times, our grandparents would take us home. It was such a blessing to have them in our lives. Because of Grandma, Brittany and I were in contact with our mother's family and we needed that closeness.

My grandparents were always together. You never saw one without the other. When the weather was good on Saturday mornings, Grandma and Pop-pop participated in the yard sale/flea market which was set up in the parking lot of Meatland, the grocery store, in Princess Anne. They would set up whatever goods they wanted to sell, and we would be there half the day. There were other people there as well with their products.

Grandma was a God-fearing lady who didn't play cards and work on Sundays. When there was thunder and lightning, she turned off most of the electrical appliances in the house. Sometimes, she even unplugged the lamps and we sat in the dark. I used to love those thunderstorm days at her house. When it stormed in the daytime and I could see, I would look at Grandma's department store catalogs and dream of the things I wished I could order from those books. I have such fond memories of those times!

I would do anything for my grandparents. I remember one time, I called myself cleaning up Grandma's living room. No, she didn't ask me to do it. I took it upon myself to help. I was about 10, and I remember I went through all her photos and everything, stacking and re-stacking them in neat piles. I laugh about it now, but Grandma was not too happy with me that day. The way she explained it was, that despite what I thought I was doing to help her, she knew where her things were because she put them there and when I took it upon myself to help and moved her things, I moved them from where she had put them, and she couldn't find them. I understood what she meant I apologized and attempted to put things back, so grandma could find her things. I loved my grandma, and I take my memories of her with me every day! She nick-named me "String Bean" when I was little because of my size and flexibility. She always called me that!

On May 10, 1994, my grandmother passed away. It was the first funeral I had ever attended. I was 11, and I didn't know how to respond. All I knew was my grandma was gone, and she was not coming back. It was difficult for me to go to sleep that night after my grandmother's funeral. I didn't cry at her funeral. It wasn't that I didn't miss her; I dearly loved her. I just didn't know how to process what had happened.

That evening, I cried and rocked myself to sleep. Before I fell asleep, I had been listening to a song by Gerald Levert entitled, "Baby Hold On To Me." Every time I hear that song today, it makes me think of my grandmother and the day of her funeral. My grandmother gave me what I was missing from my mother. No, my grandmother couldn't give me everything I was missing from my mother, but she gave me the connection I was missing. My grandmother was a quiet lady who was caring and who loved her family. She had compassion for people, and she "wore her heart on her sleeve," just like I do.

Pop-pop was a man who was very gentle with his grandchildren, and he did what he could for them. He was the only grandfather I knew and had the great pleasure of spending time with in my youth. My father's father had passed away one year prior to my birth.

My grandfather had a laugh that made you laugh! He would chuckle and smile all the time. He was a faithful worker in the church. Whether it was changing light bulbs, cutting the grass or painting, he took care of it. I used to ask him if he got paid for doing work at the church, and he would say to me, "You don't get paid for doing the Lord's work." Those were his exact words! I remember he took pride in the work he did at the church. He would spend afternoons there while Brittany and I would be home with Grandma.

At mealtime, Pop-pop would sit in the kitchen, drink his coffee and smoke his cigarettes as he sang and hummed the songs he loved. After dinner, the routine nearly was the same. He would usually sit at the table until he finished his cigarette, watch television, and call it a day!

On March 17, 2003, when I was in my sophomore year of college, Pop-pop passed away. A few days before his death, I visited him in hospice. He let me feed him his dinner. He was very weak, but he had a smile on his face. I sat with him for a long time that day. I talked with him and even took a photo with him with my flip-phone. Little did I know that would be my last time seeing him. Two days later, Pop-pop died.

My grandfather was my hero. In a world that was confusing to me, he brought me love and security. I am forever grateful to him and my grandmother. They helped make life more pleasant. I am better because they were a part of my life. I am blessed to have been able to spend so much time with them. I love them, and I dearly miss them. When I speak with some people, some don't even know their grandparents or have never had the opportunity to spend time with them. I am very fortune!

My grandparents taught me the meaning of love, family, togetherness, giving, and caring for one another. I have been blessed to have so many fond memories of times spent with them. I have a few teddy bears from my grandmother's house. Today, it is not unusual for me to fondly gaze at them and be reminded of those wonderful times my sister and I spent with grandma and Pop-pop.

7

A KISS FROM A ROSE

Seal

A Permanent Reminder

I look in the mirror and am reminded of permanent things: a dividing line that separates the North from the South and the East from the West; a parallel line that separates good and evil; and a permanent fixture which remains day after day.

I stare at the scar on my forehead. It looks the same as it looked yesterday, and the day before, and the day before. It is permanent. That scar and the scars on my legs are forever reminders of the night of October 28, 1987 and the tragic accident which forever changed my life.

For years, this scar affected my self-esteem. The pain I felt when cruel children at school called me "Scar-face" was unbearable. They didn't know my story.

I've tried to hide this scar for more than three decades. I had worn scarves and hats to try to conceal a portion of my face. I've tried make-up and even different hair styles; however, nothing seems to change the permanence of this scar.

I have pondered this scar for a long time. What do people think? What will people say? Why does it look like this? Can it be removed? Should I remove it? Will I look the same? Will I look better or worse? How will I ultimately feel? Will removing it help my self-esteem? After all those questions, I asked myself the ultimate and most important question: Will it remove the last 30 years of my life?

I concluded that this scar on my face, as well as the scars on my legs, tell a story about my life. Without me ever uttering a word, it tells a story about my mother and my sister and their deaths. It tells about my little sister, Brittany and my dad.

Pain, loss, anger, sadness, emptiness, struggle, and endurance are the components of this scar which I deem not so gorgeous.

Although I think about the scar, no one asks me about it. Only when I point it out do people ask me about it. Yet, I am very self-conscious about my scar. Sometimes, I hate taking pictures. I often try to sit and take pictures at different angles to prevent the scar from being seen. Sometimes, I am embarrassed and will take several pictures of the same pose until I like one that does not show my scar. The scars on my legs don't bother me as much unless I wear shorts and dresses.

Perhaps, I should view my scars as kisses from God. He spared my life and left me here to remind someone that despite trials and tribulations, He will help you to endure loss and pain.

Changes

When he looked at the total chaos in his community, the artist, Tupac Shakur, in his song, "Changes," said, "We gotta start makin'changes." Well, it was 1995, and another big change was on the horizon for Brittany and me because some things in our lives were out of order.

One day, during the summer, while Brittany and I were at home in the fourth house we had lived in since moving to Princess Anne, a social worker arrived to check on our welfare. My dad had gone to work, and Brittany and I were home alone because Dad's girlfriend had moved her six kids to her mother's home. We didn't have electricity, and the only sounds in the house were produced by a small battery-operated radio I had. Evidently, someone had called Social Services and told them that my sister and I were not being properly cared for and someone should pay us a visit.

I don't know who made the call; however, I remember a few days before the social worker came, one of my paternal aunts brought lunch to the house for Brittany and me. She had done this on other occasions as well. At the time, I didn't realize how bad the situation looked. The social worker determined it was not good. That day, the Department of Social Services removed Brittany and me from the house. I was 11, and Brittany was 8.

Smile!

Thinking of this time in my life, I think of the words of Michael Jackson's song, "Smile."

> Smile though your heart is aching
>
> Smile even though it's breaking.
>
> When there are clouds in the sky
>
> You'll get by if you smile.

Through the chaos. I managed to smile! There were so many changes taking place in my life. After Social Services took Britany and me away from our father, it was apparent they had not thought about where we were going to live. With God looking out for us, Brittany and I went to stay a few days at a time and sometimes, a few weeks with Pop-Pop. We loved him and because we had stayed many times with our grandparents, it was natural for us to stay him now. It was a little hard staying with Pop-Pop at first because I was used to seeing my grandmother in the house. Grandma died a year prior to us returning to the house in Fairmount.

More than two decades later, this period in my life makes me sad. When we first left my father's house, we had nowhere to go and my grandfather, an elderly man in his 70's, took on the care of Brittany and me. I am blessed to have had such a wonderful grandfather in my life.

Pop-Pop lived mostly alone, except when my Aunt Kim came home from college. He didn't have much, but he was willing to share what he had with his orphaned and neglected grandchildren. Until the day he died, my Pop-pop probably had no idea what he did for us. He is my Hero!

During this time, I didn't have the best clothes because I simply had no one who could get me those things. I had to wear to school what I had been given. My clothing wasn't the latest and the greatest styles like the kids at school were wearing, but I had clothes and I was warm.

One day, a so-called friend asked me, "What are you wearing?" She was laughing at me. What I was wearing did not meet her approval. I was hurt by her comment, even though I never mentioned it to her. I just kept a smile on my face to hide the hurt. It's funny how God turns things around. Occasionally, I am in contact with this person today, and all I am going to say is that it's funny how the tables turn! I would never want to trade places with her. Life has a way of paying us back for things we do and say to and about others.

The teasing about my clothes continued in middle school. Most of the time, as I was being teased, I laughed along with the other children. It was the only way I knew to cover my pain. How crazy was that behavior? My self-esteem was low! In fact, I had none. It's funny how, today, I see some of those same people who teased me. I notice life has not treated them especially well. We do reap what we sow.

No one at school knew the life I was living at home. No one knew I always felt lost because my mother was gone and now my father was gone. Things were out of my control, and all I could do as a child was keep moving and allow the adults to be adults and work out the details of my life.

After my short stay at my grandfather's home, I went to stay with my maternal aunt with whom I had stayed when I was released from the hospital after the accident. She and her husband still lived in Princess Anne; therefore, I didn't have to move far.

I was grateful for the new living arrangement where I had my own space. To have someone who would take care of me and buy me the things I needed was wonderful. There were no more days of being hungry or waiting to see if I would get new shoes because the shoes I was wearing did not belong to me and didn't fit.

Living with my aunt and uncle allowed me to regularly see my cousins and my mother's family. Brittany was taken to live not too far away with another of my mother's sisters, in Marion, MD. This arrangement allowed me to see Brittany whenever I wanted to see her; this was great!

The home of my aunt and uncle was very quiet. It was quite different than the environment I had shared with my father, his girlfriend, and six children. I was used to kids running all over the place, rap music, loud talking, and a little cussing.

Though I was grateful to have food and shelter, I still had a difficult time adjusting. Oftentimes, I spend a lot of time alone in my room, listening to music by myself. In my room was where I felt close to my dreams; it was my happy place. I enjoyed the solitude.

Seemingly, there was a communication issue between my aunt and me. She did things one way, and I did things another way. Sometimes, I rebelled when I was corrected. Yes, at times, I had an attitude. I had been through a lot, and I wasn't always ready to recognize how my aunt preferred things to be done. Sometimes, I incorrectly did things because I hadn't been given any guidelines. I simply did them the way I had always done them.

After six months of trying to live together, the lines of communication between my aunt and me had not improved. Stress was taking its toll on my aunt, and she concluded I probably would fare better in a different environment. Thus, I was sent to live in a foster home at the end of the sixth grade. I was 12 years of age.

Living in a Foster Home

What was a Foster Home? As soon as I heard the term, I looked in the dictionary to get an understanding. It didn't take me long to learn this was a place where an orphaned, neglected or delinquent child is placed for care. Immediately, I wondered if I would be moving in a house with nice people. Where did they live? Would I be able to see Brittany? I had so many questions.

Moving into a foster home meant I would have to again adjust to a new living arrangement, new rules, and new people whom I did not know. I guess I can say the one good thing about this experience was my foster home was walking distance from the home of my aunt and uncle whom I had just left. Even though I had left their home, I still loved them and appreciated what they had tried to do for me. I knew I could visit them from time to time.

Sometimes, you hear horror stories about foster parents neglecting and mistreating children. This was not the case for me. I was fortunate! My foster mother was a single mother whose only daughter was a few years younger than I. This lady was kind and caring. She treated me like a daughter. While living with my foster mother, I regularly attended church, school events, and field trips. I had a normal life with stability.

Even with the stability of living in a comfortable home, from time to time, I rocked to comfort myself. I guess, moving from place to place was taking its toll. It was a blessing I wasn't crazy!

Not long after I was placed in foster care, my aunt and uncle who were caring for Brittany became overwhelmed trying to care for her. Brittany's disability required that she be cared for twenty-four hours a day. My aunt and uncle tried their best; however, they were not physically equipped to care for Brittany.

Brittany was placed in a foster home in Snow Hill, MD. It was a bit of a distance from where I lived in Princess Anne. There were several other children who lived in Brittany's new residence. The foster family my sister went to live with had several other kids. Sometimes, during my visits to see her, I didn't feel my sister was being taken care in a proper manner. I couldn't prove anything; I only had this feeling.

Self-Esteem? Where?

I didn't feel pretty. I didn't like my big forehead with the scar, my full lips, and my button nose. I didn't have the name-brand clothes everyone was wearing, and because of this, my feelings were hurt a lot of times by my so-called friends. I felt the lowest of the low. Kids were cruel.

One bright light during my middle school years was the presence in my life of my therapist and my social worker, Miss Rounds.

Miss Rounds entered my life when I was approximately 11 years old. She made sure Brittany and I received the proper care. She not only took me to appointments to meet my dad, but she also took me to my doctor's appointments when I was in foster care. When Miss Rounds arrived to take me to my appointments, I always asked for snacks. She never denied my requests.

Miss Rounds helped make the transition from my aunt's home to my new foster home an easy one. I have no idea how I would have gotten through those days if it hadn't been for people like her who were there for me.

During this time, my father lost all rights to Brittany and me; we became wards of the state. A ward of the state is someone placed under protection of a legal guardian. A court may take responsibility for the legal protection of an individual, usually a child.

Miss Rounds arranged for us to meet with our father at the Department of Social Services, in Princess Anne. When we met with him, Brittany's foster mother would bring her to the meetings. Sometimes, my dad didn't come as planned. Those times were very disappointing for us because we were excited and anxious to see him.

We needed our father. He was the only parent we had and when he didn't show up, we were sad as we returned to our foster homes. This sadness added fuel to the anger which had been building up within me for a few years as his care for Brittany and me declined. For God's sake, we were his children! Why did he not come? Did he not love us? Little did I know, my dad was fighting his own personal battles. This realization came years later. As a child, all I knew was my father whom I thought loved us, seemingly did not love us enough to be present in our lives. After my dad failed to come to several meetings, I had to accept reality. Each time a visit was scheduled, I knew I either would feel happy or I would feel defeated.

8

A DEEPER LOVE

Aretha Franklin

The Music Therapy Continues

Aretha Franklin said, "It's the power that gives you the strength to survive." For me, the power was music!

Among some of my favorite artists at the time were TLC, SWV, Jade, Mary J. Blige and Jodeci. At this time, I had started a little hobby of writing the words to some of my favorite songs in a book. I learned "You're All I Need" by Mary J. Blige & Method Man. I had the RAP down to that song! One of my favorite lines was, "Shorty, I'm there for you anytime you need me, for real girl, it's me in your world believe me."

TLC was an extremely popular group in 1996, and I loved one of their albums which included: "Diggin' on You," "Case of the Fake People," and "Creep." My foster mother's daughter, a girl from the neighbor, and I would pretend we were TLC. I was Left-Eye (Lisa Lopes), my favorite singer in the group.

Music was a powerful influence in my world as I daydreamed away the time. Reality was too harsh for me; pretending was a better fit. At least living in the foster home, I had someone who loved music like I did and didn't mind playing along with my desire to escape my real world.

9

THROW OUT THE LIFE LINE

Ella Fitzgerald

The Move Which Changed My Life

In the summer of 1996, I left my foster home after living there for almost two years. Leaving was a bitter-sweet experience because I had been treated exceptionally well by my foster mother and her daughter. On the other hand, I was excited about the invitation extended to me by one of my father's sisters and her husband who lived in Salisbury. This couple, Aunt Gloria and Uncle Kenneth, wanted me to come to live with them. That summer, I turned 14, and they welcomed me with open arms. This was such a blessing!

I am forever grateful for the decision they made to allow me to stay with them and I love them more than they will ever know.

Because I had known Aunt Gloria and Uncle Kenneth my entire life, moving in with them was easy because a closeness had already existed between us. When my mother was living, she and Aunt Gloria were more like sisters than in-laws. They were both pregnant at the same time and were good friends. Aunt Gloria's daughter, Megan, and I were born just two days apart. We even resembled each other to the extent people thought we were sisters. In addition to Megan, my aunt and uncle had two other children who were older than Megan.

Megan and I got along well. We had played together so much when we were much younger that it was a natural process when we began to live together. Whatever my aunt brought for Megan, she brought for me! Whatever activities Megan was involved in, I was involved in as well: church youth choir, church dance group, church drill team, hand-bell choir, school dances, school band, piano lessons and football games.

One activity in which both Megan and I were involved in and thoroughly enjoyed was Sisterhood, a program designed for female pre-teens and teenagers. The founder and director of Sisterhood was Mrs. Rachel Polk, a community activist and the owner of Grassroots, an African-American bookstore, in Salisbury. We met once a month to learn and understand the complexities of the female body and how a lady should behave and not behave in public. We also learned the history of Africa and took interesting field trips. One trip was to the Million Woman March, in Philadelphia. Then, every year, on December 26, we participated in a Kwanzaa program.

At the end of the year, young ladies who were ready to advance to a higher level in their journey toward womanhood, were tested on the information they had been exposed to while being in the program. If they successfully passed the test, they were eligible to participate in the Rights of Passage. This was an exciting event which signified their exit from childhood and their entrance into womanhood.

While living with Aunt Gloria and Uncle Kenneth, I was very blessed to have regular and routine access to doctors and dentists. When I was younger, other than the time I lived in the foster home and at my maternal aunt's home, doctor appointments were rare.

Many valuable lessons were taught to me by my aunt and uncle. The first lesson I learned was to finish whatever I started. Before I decided to quit my piano lessons, I had become proficient enough to participate in recitals. However, I became bored and had no desire to continue practicing. I quit! My aunt said to me, "In life, you don't ever want to start something and not finish it. Don't be a quitter." I heard Aunt Gloria; however, I had no desire to resume the piano lessons. I was finished with that project. For the future, though, I knew I needed to take to heart what she told me. From that day until this day, I complete whatever I began.

My aunt and uncle taught me to set priorities. Even though I was involved in many activities, Aunt Gloria and Uncle Kenneth reminded me of the importance of putting my education first. They monitored my academic progress and stressed the advantage of maintaining a high-grade point average. Neither fair nor poor grades were what they wanted to see on my report card. I learned to multi-task in order to participate in the many activities I loved and to maintain my grades at the same time.

Another great value my aunt and uncle instilled in me was the importance of putting God first in my life. Along with them, I had to regularly attend church. Being out a little late on Saturday night was not a reason to not be in church on Sunday morning!

Like me, my aunt and uncle were family-oriented. They enjoyed and participated whenever there was an occasion for our immediate and extended family to gather. Oftentimes, my father didn't attend these functions. His absence was difficult to understand because the people who attended these events was his family.

Where I Got Lost

Because of the many changes which had occurred in my life, relaxing was not easy for me. It was always in the back of my mind, if I did anything my aunt and uncle didn't like, they would send me back to the foster home. Now, my aunt and uncle never said or did anything that should have made me feel this way. For some crazy reason, I just thought this could happen. To prevent being sent away, I began to imitate my cousins. If whatever they did was alright, then, I figured it was alright for me to do it as well.

Megan and I lived in the same house; therefore, it was easier for me to imitate whatever she did. If she wanted pizza, I wanted pizza. If she preferred wearing a dress, Stephanie would wear a dress. It didn't matter that I didn't like wearing dresses. I became someone other than myself; I lost my identity.

This new-found role I played caused me to deny my true self. Not wanting to be rejected, I decided to survive by being someone else. I mimicked other people's opinions about everything. I stopped sharing my thoughts because I didn't want to run the risk of someone disagreeing with me and thinking my opinions were of no value. It was not that I didn't have an opinion, I just didn't want to share it and it be considered wrong. I didn't want to make any mistakes! I was lost!

10

YOU GETS NO LOVE

Faith Evans

He Loves Me, He Loves Me Not

I felt no love for myself and wondered if anybody loved me. This love thing was something I wanted; however, I couldn't seem to connect with it. The first time I was in love was in kindergarten when I was 5. I fell in love with Josh Perkins, a little boy whose smile blew me away! Did he love me? I don't know. Then, when I was 8, in the second grade for the second time, I was smitten by Todd Johnson! According to our plans, he and I were going to get married under the tree on the playground at school! We were serious!

In the eighth grade, Travis fell in love with me. I was fascinated by him and our love lasted four days: two days at the beginning of the year and two days at the end of the year. In between those days, there was Toby. He was kind of tough and strong; I liked that in a boy! He and I didn't talk too much; however, that was okay. I was grateful for a little attention.

During high school, I was prone to be attracted to popular guys who were not attracted to me. As far as dates were concerned, I had very, very few of them. I dated one boy, Marcus, whom I met the summer before my senior year. He and I worked at Wendy's. He was nice, but I was not smitten!

Senior Year Struggles

My senior year in high school began September 2000. I should have graduated with Megan in June 2000, but my failure in the second grade caused me to be a year behind my class. I loved the class of 2000, and I had a blast when I attended their prom in my junior year. My senior year was a year I just wanted to end. I had no interest in attending any school events; I just wanted to graduate. I wasn't even looking forward to going to the prom. I only wanted to see June 2001.

Megan was in her freshman year of college and as I journeyed through my senior year, she schooled me about what to expect from college. The fact that I was going to attend college was a no-brainer for me. My aunt, uncle, and Megan made sure I was prepared for school. They made sure I took the college tests and correctly completed the applications. I was excited about college!

Two months prior to my high school graduation, just when it seemed as if my life were on an upswing, I suffered a terrible loss. On April 16, 2001, a few minutes before midnight, Brittany had a seizure while she was asleep. At the age of 15, my baby sister was gone! This was a major blow for me.

Since the October 1987 accident, Brittany had taken medicine to control the seizures she suffered because of her brain damage. On the day Brittany died, she had undergone a surgery procedure to remove a mole that was thought to be cancerous. She had the procedure early in the day and returned to her place of residence where she died that night.

At the time of her death, Brittany was no longer with her foster parents because they could not adequately provide for her. She lived at the Brickhouse Group Home, in Elkton, Maryland, a facility which was equipped to handle her special needs. At one time, Brittany had been a resident of the Holly Center, in Salisbury, and a student at the Marion Sarah Peyton School for the developmentally challenged.

The night my sister died, I had an unusual dream in which Brittany and I were sitting and having a conversation. In reality, Brittany could not verbally communicate with me. When I received the call about Brittany's death, I remembered the dream. I strongly believe that before someone whom we love dies, God sends us signs. Sometimes, we don't recognize these signs until after our loved one dies. Could it have been my sister was telling me she was leaving me? I honestly believe this to be true.

My plan, after graduating from high school and college, was to have Brittany come and live with me. She was like my child, and I loved her as no sister could ever love their sister. Though the people who worked with my sister knew Brittany had a father, they had never met him. They had, however, met me many times because I would go to see Brittany and check on her surroundings and the people who cared for her. I even met her teachers.

In my sister's room at the Brickhouse Group Home, I left pictures of family members and some personal items. I wanted Brittany to have something to which she could relate.

A few months prior to Brittany's death, I was given an unexpected opportunity to visit my sister, in Elkton. This was during the Christmas holiday, and I had not done my shopping for Brittany. I had planned to bring her gifts with me when I visited her after her surgery. Little did I know, what I thought was an unexpected opportunity, would be my last opportunity to see my sister alive.

The loss of my sister affected me in a way I can't describe. In addition to the overwhelming sadness, I was confronted with the fact that there was no money to bury Brittany. There was no insurance policy, and my father and I were financially unable to even start the process of Brittany's burial. Thankfully, I have a wonderful family who came together to help bury my sister. The support on both my father's side of the family and my mother's side of the family helped provide the money that was needed to lay Brittany to rest. God is good!

The day of Brittany's funeral, I was numb. I couldn't believe this was happening. In Brittany's obituary, she was described as a very affectionate, loving child towards those who loved her. So true! The obituary also stated how she loved to hum, sing, and clap her hands. Everyone laughed when it was said, above all else, Brittany loved to eat. God knows, we needed a light moment in the midst of our grief for many hearts were heavy that April morning as we did our best to bid farewell to an exceptional and remarkable little girl whom God had lent to us for fifteen years.

I had not attended my mother's and Autumn's funeral service because I was hospitalized. As we stood in the cemetery to lower Brittany's casket into the ground, I couldn't help but to see the graves of my mother and my sister. Brittany was buried right beside them. But for the mercy of God, this day would have overwhelmed me beyond anything I could have imagined. Such sadness!

This was an extremely emotional time for my father and for me. Mentally, it was difficult for him to handle. He had just buried his second child. I knew I had to stay as mentally alert as possible because someone had to handle the business of death. Again, I thank God for my family.

Although I was feeling so much pain and anguish, I found joy in receiving my sister's belongings: art work, school work, photos, and her clothes. I even received a burial plaque the funeral home prepared for grieving families.

After handling my sister's funeral, I still needed to make sure I graduated on time. I was close to failing my Chemistry CM class which was a requirement for graduation. With God's help, I passed the class and graduated June 2001!

I guess God looked at me and knew I needed a blessing. It came in the form of the decision my Aunt Gloria and Uncle Kenneth made about my future. They decided to adopt me! This act of kindness meant I was no longer a ward of the state. Though I was 18, an age usually considered too old for adoption, my aunt and uncle still moved forward with the process. No longer were my biological parents listed as my parents; my aunt and uncle assumed that role. I do, of course, have a copy of my original birth certificate.

At the court house, during the adoption procedures, I was asked if I wanted to change my last name. I declined because I had always been a WHITE and changing my last name would have meant I was changing who I was and had been for the last eighteen years of my life.

I am grateful to Aunt Gloria and Uncle Kenneth who acted so selflessly and took me not only into their home, but into their hearts. With my adoption, I acquired three siblings. Now, Megan and I were really sisters!

11

FREEDOM
Pharrell Williams

The College Years

Although I had been preparing to attend college, my focus had been on how to care for Brittany. Now, Brittany was gone. I had to make a mental shift. It wasn't easy because I thought a lot about the deaths of my two sisters, and truthfully, I felt as if my demise was next! I was the only one of my mother's children still alive. This was a frightening reality! Despite how I felt, I knew my thinking had to change because I was still alive and had to move on with life. Freedom from my dismal outlook was what I needed.

In September 2001, I enrolled at the University of Maryland Eastern Shore, in Princess Anne. Even though I decided to live off-campus and commute the twenty minutes to school every day, being present on the campus opened a whole new world for me. New friends and new experiences equaled new freedom! This new atmosphere was the place where I began to re-discover my true self. No longer was I totally focused on the past; a new world lay at my feet.

When I enrolled at UMES, my major was Social Work. This decision was based on my concern for children whose lives had been turned upside down due to circumstances beyond their control. It did not take me long to realize this major wasn't the best match for me because I feared becoming overwhelmingly attached to people's emotions and problems. I would have taken their troubles with me wherever I would have gone. I knew their pain would have resonated with me, and I would not have been able to cope. I quickly switched my major to Business Administration before I invested any more time pursuing a degree in Social Work. This was a very smart decision on my part.

The Greatest Love of All

At the age 19, I didn't know who Stephanie was, what Stephanie liked, and what Stephanie disliked. For as long as I could remember, my choices had been made based on someone else's opinion. Stephanie didn't have a voice! This had to change!

The change began during my freshman year. I was determined to be myself! I was "rocking" straight permed hair and sporting Air-Force One sneakers which were popular. I jumped on the Roca-Wear clothing band wagon, along with the MAC Make-up wagon! Though others were wearing some of the same fashions, the decision I made to indulge in the style was a decision I made for myself. To say that my freshman year was fun and interesting is an understatement.

When I attended UMES, Uncle Kenneth was employed at Salisbury State University, a school within the University of Maryland System. Because of his status as a University of Maryland System employee, his children were eligible to receive free tuition at any school within the University of Maryland System and my adoptive status made me eligible as well. This was a blessing I didn't see coming.

Because I lived at home while in college, I had no need for a school loan! I was, however, eligible for a school grant which I received in the form of a refund check.

It would have made more sense if I had saved that money, but my mind was on shopping! I couldn't wait to cross the Chesapeake Bay Bridge and shop in Western Maryland and Washington, DC. I was making my own way! Whitney Houston, in her song, "Greatest Love of All," said, "Learning to love yourself, it is the greatest love of all." I guess this is what was happening to me: I was learning to love myself. It was a good feeling!

At the age of 19, like any teenager, I was curious about sex. In a conversation with a friend of mines, I mentioned I was a virgin. She said to me, "Who you lose your virginity to should be someone you consider to be special." This wasn't the first time I had heard this comment. To myself, I was thinking, "Yeah! Okay!" As far as I was concerned, everybody's story probably was different. Eventually, what my friend said didn't satisfy my curiosity because I felt it was past time for me to have lost my virginity. I don't know why I thought I had a deadline to accomplish this great moment in life! Well, you know the rest of the story. I lost my virginity! Ironically, my partner-in-crime was a guy from the *City of Brotherly Love*, Philadelphia! Philly! There was nothing special about the moment. I was just curious! We did it; I experienced how it felt, and I moved on! No regrets!!

I continued to find my way back to my authentic self. It wasn't always easy because in the process of working on myself, there were people who wanted to use me for their benefit. I decided if they used me once, it was to their shame. If I allowed them to use me again, it was to my shame.

Sometimes, in attempts to fit in with my peers, I found myself returning to old behaviors. As opposed to doing what I wanted to do, I did what they wanted to do. Initially, I felt weird as I tried to decipher between my voice and the voices of others. What others thought of me was important; however, I had to remind myself of my need to be myself. I told myself, "It's alright to like things no one else likes. If you want to go left when everybody else is going right, that is not a problem. Your opinion matters just like the next person's opinion matters. It's okay to not like dresses. This doesn't make you a boy because you don't want to put on a dress. It's okay to be an individual." This business of trying to love myself was hard work.

My freshman year at UMES was successful, and in September 2002, I eagerly entered my sophomore year. Pursuing more freedom, I purchased my first car! A 2001 silver Dodge Neon! My monthly payment was $163.81. I loved that car! Her name was Lana! To purchase the car, I needed a co-signer. I made sure every payment was made on time; I was not in the business of messing up anyone's credit!

During my sophomore year, I continued to work part-time at The Home Depot Hardware Store. This was a job I started the second half of my freshman year. I worked four days a week: Tuesday, Thursday, Saturday and Sunday. I kept this job for the remainder of my college years and did whatever I was asked to do including making keys, mixing paint and operating the terminal as a returns certified cashier!

Because I didn't live on campus, it took an extra effort for me to attend events on campus. This, however, did not prevent me from being involved in numerous activities. For example, I volunteered to help back-stage with the Drama Club's production of **The Wizard of Oz**. I enjoyed working with the cast and crew. Being with them made me wonder what it would be like to live on campus. Then, I made peace with the fact that living on campus might have been too much of a distraction for me because I needed quietness in which to focus on my studies.

During my junior year, I took classes in Sales and Marketing and joined the American Marketing Association Club on campus. This allowed me the opportunity to interact with other Business Administration students. In the AMA Club, we planned events and raised money for our organization.

Determined to graduate on time, I took classes during the summer and winter breaks. I was determined to finish my degree in four years and that's what I did! In May 2005, I graduated with a Bachelor of Science degree in Business Administration with a Concentration in Marketing.

What a beautiful day as I was congratulated by family and friends! Many people who knew my story and had been with me during the journey were present that day, including my social worker, Miss Rounds and my foster mother. I was delighted to see my father that afternoon. As always, when he saw me, a broad smile crossed his face. I knew he was proud of me.

12

WELCOME TO DC

Mambo Sauce

Welcome to DC

When opportunity knocks, you answer! A month after graduation, Megan, who had recently graduated from the University of Maryland College Park and was living in College Park, MD, a city close to Washington, DC, invited me to come and live with her. Without hesitation, I accepted her invitation because I did not want to allow myself time to think about why I shouldn't make the move. My future was in front of me, and I was ready for a new adventure. I packed my belongings in my 2001 Dodge Neon and headed to the BIG CITY!

I shared a three-bedroom, two-bathroom apartment in a high-rise with Megan and her roommate and college friend, Leon. Our apartment was on the 17th Floor. What a view of the city!

Three's Company

As I observed the dynamics of our household, I remembered how Jack, Janet, and Chrissy, the characters in the sitcom, **Three's Company**, operated. They moved through life existing as a unit, but also as individuals. They did things together, and they did things separately. Jack always had his ladies; Chrissy always had her men, and Janet was busy doing whatever Janet loved to do.

Megan, Leon and I often operated in the same fashion. Some things, we did together. Other things, we did separately. Rent was split three ways, and we shared some of the food. There were times, however, when we kept our food separate. I spent a lot of time in my room, enjoying watching television. Leon spent a lot of time in the living room, and Megan spent time in both her room and the living room.

I shared a bathroom with Leon. My bedroom had an entry door to the balcony, and this was more important to me than having my own bathroom. Sharing a bathroom taught me how to share my space and to be a better communicator.

When I moved to College Park, I was unemployed. I had some money in my bank account and with that, I paid my share of the rent and brought gas for my car. Later that year, I was hired part-time as a Bridal Hostess at Martin's Crosswinds, in Greenbelt, MD. I loved that job! It was my introduction to the Wedding and Hospitality Industry.

Happy, But Gullible

I was happy being on my own! Gradually, I began to meet people who lived in my building. One day, I met Norman who mentioned that he worked for a mortuary. He seemed like a "cool dude." Oftentimes, I would go with him to different places. He seemed harmless. Norman and I were hanging out one day, and he told me that he was having some issues with his bank and wanted me to cash some checks! I agree to cash two checks for him. They were bad checks! Lo and behold, Norman, my "cool" and "harmless friend" scammed me to the tune of $800.00! I had no idea Norman was lying to me! My bank came after me for that money. This naïve and gullible young woman was in a world of trouble. I did not have that money to repay the bank, and it seemed as if Norman had disappeared from the face of the earth! Nowhere to be found! I didn't know what to do, but God had the answer!

Aunt B. to the Rescue!

My Aunt B. was one of my mother's sisters who had lived and worked as an educator and a writer for more than thirty years, in Prince George's County, MD, near Washington, DC. I had no idea what to do about the money I had lost; therefore, I reached out to Aunt B. and told her about the situation with Norman. My aunt said to me, "I think I know his parents!" Now, in a county with a population of 840, 513 people, what are the odds of my aunt knowing Norman's parents? But God!

My aunt reached out to Norman's mother who was very upset by what my aunt told her had happened. I guess she knew her son was capable of such dishonest behavior, and when she questioned him, he admitted to what he had done. She contacted me and arranged to pay her son's debt. I felt sorry for her because she couldn't afford to give me all the money at one time; we agreed she could make payments. True to her word, she paid the $800.00. God was really looking out for me, and I learned three valuable lessons: always think before lending money; don't be so quick to say YES, and to the best of your ability, check the background of people before you get close to them.

Me + Me = Me

After being hired by Martin's crosswinds, I

was hired by a Temp Agency. Although I was working two jobs, I still had time for socializing. Most of the time, I hung out with Megan. What I forgot to realize was Megan had her own life, and I should not have expected her to entertain me all the time. This fact became abundantly clear one afternoon when I arrived home early from work and Megan's friends were at the apartment. They were planning to go out together. Because I usually went out with Megan, I naturally assumed I would be invited to go with the group. There was no invitation! They all left without me. I was hurt and cried a little.

From that day forward, I vowed to never again allow another human being to make me feel the way I felt that day. I dried my eyes, got dressed, and moved on with my evening. I was on a mission to meet new people and create my own circle of friends. I held on to that experience in my mind for years. It was a constant reminder to me to not depend on others to entertain me or do anything for me for that matter. Years later, I mentioned this incident to Megan, and she didn't even remember the incident to which I referred. I guess the moral to this story is when you have a problem, you need to immediately address it. Don't hold on to it for years and years, like I did.

13

IT'S A NEW SEASON
Israel and New Breed

New Church, New Beginning, New Season

My family were Christians, and I had grown up in the United Methodist Church. When I moved to College Park, I began attending Reid Temple African American Episcopal Church with Megan. Every Sunday, she and I attended the 6 PM service for the young people.

When I attended church, it was because it was something that had been instilled in me many years ago; it was tradition. I went to church out of habit. Yes, I prayed to God, enjoyed and sang along with the church choir and even followed along in the Bible when the word was being read at church. With all of this, I just felt like I was going through the motions. Now, don't get me wrong. My prayers to God were true and real, but the rest was habit. I can't say I truly had a relationship with God in the same way others told me that they had with Him. I wanted something like they had with God. I wanted my own personal relationship with Him, the One to whom I prayed. Based on this longing, I decided to take this church thing seriously.

Desiring to draw nearer to God, I went to service every Sunday morning. I became serious about reading the Bible and paid close attention to what the pastor preached. I took notes and sometimes, I would review them when I got home. My church family became my family and a part of my everyday life.

Wanting to be active in the church, I joined the Singles Ministry. It was a joy to learn God's plan for singles and how to be satisfied in my singleness. To mingle with other singles was an amazing experience because we all wanted to please God.

Reid Temple AME Church, which I joined in 2007, is often described as a mega-church because it has well over six thousand members. Attending such a church can be overwhelming for someone who is used to a smaller, more intimate setting. To engage and support all members of the church, the church created a Class Leaders Ministry. The members of the church are assigned a Class Leader who helps them stay connected with other church members in their class on a more intimate level.

I became an assistant to one of the Class Leaders and dutifully contacted the members of my class every month, attended monthly class leader meetings, gave updates, and planned class functions. This ministry gave me the opportunity to meet more members of the church and expand my church family circle. After a few years, my desire and excitement for the Class Leaders Ministry and the Singles Ministry diminished, and I was ready to try something else.

I always enjoyed working with youth, and I was blessed with several opportunities to plan and facilitate workshops for youth in other organizations at church. This interest in youth led me to join the Christian Debutante's Ministry at Reid Temple where I became a volunteer helper. Interestingly, the leader of this ministry was a lady whom I had met during my employment as a Bridal Hostess. She was serious about helping and developing the youth of the church.

The purpose of the Christian Debutante's Ministry was to prepare female youth, ages 10-17, for various areas of life. For example, the young people were instructed about the pros and cons of social media, ways to read the Bible, and how to properly care for themselves. The ladies were taken on field trips and encouraged to participate in community service events planned by the ministry leader. It was my responsible to attend class each month and help wherever needed. Sometimes, I taught a class.

For the four years I was a member of this ministry, I enjoyed working with the youth at Reid Temple because I was able to mentor them and help in their development. This was my way of giving back for all I had received during my lifetime. When the kids began to learn my name and ask me for help, this was rewarding because it meant I was making a difference in their lives.

By Summer 2008, I had moved into my own apartment and was working full-time. My Dodge Neon had seen better days; therefore, I traded "her" in for a 2008 Honda Accord! Life was good! I was independent and content!

Nobody Greater

A year after joining Reid Temple, I continued to focus on developing a deeper walk with God. At this stage in my life when I was totally responsible for taking care of myself, I needed God more than ever. This is not to say I didn't need God during my youth. The difference between then and now was that, in my youth, the adults were responsible for taking care of me. I'm sure some of them sought God's help in caring for me. Now, I had to seek God for myself.

All my life, I have had an awareness of God. I remember praying a lot when I was a child, but I don't think I completely understood to whom I was praying or even if anyone was listening. I just knew to pray. I prayed for things to happen and for people to come to enhance my life. Often, I prayed for another mother for Brittany and me. It was not that I didn't love my father; I just missed having a mother. Usually, I wanted immediate answers to my prayers. Little did I know, God was watching every moment of my life, saving me from situations and circumstances that were out of my control.

As I grew closer to God, He sent people to help me along my spiritual journey. One of the first people whom I knew was God-sent was a Christian sister who took me under her wing when I joined the Singles Ministry. This sister introduced me to a circle of wonderful woman at the church. Many of these women and I became like family. Until this day, we stay in contact and support each other. These friendships are extremely valuable to me because, during my earlier years, I never had the opportunity to develop long-lasting friendships because of having to constantly move from place to place.

Although I had joined the church, I wasn't sure if I had ever been baptized. When I asked my father about my baptism, he wasn't sure if it had ever occurred. That answer wasn't good enough for me! Not knowing troubled me because I felt baptism was a very important part of my walk with God. This walk with God had to be right!

Getting my walk right brings me to a date I will never forget. I even write it in an unforgettable way: 10.10.10. This was my date of baptism at Reid Temple AME Church! October 10, 2010! Totally submerged in water! I wanted my Senior Pastor to baptize me; however, he was not available that day. I was fine with whomever baptized me that beautiful October afternoon. My baptism was an outward sign I had accepted Christ Jesus as my Lord and Savior! I was blessed, and I knew God was pleased. That day reminds me of the words of "Nobody Greater" by gospel artist, VaShawn Mitchell:

"Searched all over – couldn't find nobody

I looked high and low – still couldn't find nobody

Nobody greater, nobody greater - no

Nobody greater than You."

Generally, when someone has an important event in their life, they will first call their family and invite them to celebrate their great accomplishment. For some unknown reason, it never dawned on me to invite my family to my baptism. Yes, they would have come. I did, however, think to ask the circle of women whom I had met and bonded with at church. These ladies became my spiritual sounding boards, my sisters, and my friends.

14

GONNA BE A
LOVELY DAY

Kirk Franklin

Knowing & Learning God for Myself

After my baptism, I continued to grow in my relationship with God. I was determined to stay focused and not straddle the fence. In other words, I did not want to have one foot in the church and one foot in the world. At a point, I became rigid. When I say *rigid*, I mean *rigid*! I didn't step to the right or the left; I stayed right in the middle! No sex! No drugs! No cussing!

Other than for spending time with family members who didn't seem to be on a spiritual journey, I spent time with people who were seeking God. I don't mean to sound harsh; however, being selective about the company I kept was the only way I could concentrate on what I needed to learn in church and from the Bible. I had to stay in the middle and stay grounded because I still was a "babe in Christ." I wasn't strong enough to take my eyes off God. I was a student, and God was my teacher. The expression I love to use for this period in my life is "I was all in." In other words, I was deep in my dedication to God. I wanted to only live as he wanted me to live. Nothing else mattered! Being "all in" has become a way of life for me. Whatever I do, I want to give it my all.

As I sought God and wrestled with life, Aunt B. accompanied me on the journey. Instrumental in my spiritual growth, she prayed with me, talked me off "ledges," spent an abundance of time with me, and talked to me during times when I was depressed about the state of my life.

My aunt was instrumental in helping me see God's plan. When I was unemployed, she never let me lose hope. When I didn't know how to deal with certain people and situations, she read scriptures with me. One of the gifts she gave me was **The Holy Bible: Woman Thou Art Loosed!** This Bible, edited by Bishop T.D. Jakes, was a book we turned to many times to seek God's solutions to my concerns. When I needed to be uplifted, I would remember Aunt B.'s words and the scriptures she shared with me.

My aunt may never truly know the impact she has made on my life and the impact her words have made as I sought God. It was a strong impact! I am forever grateful to her and I dearly love her! She and I are extremely close, and we share a very special spiritual connection.

My relationship with God involved Him showing me in dreams, solutions to problems. One such dream occurred, in 2010. I recently had graduated from the University of Maryland College Park with a Master of Science degree in Management with Marketing, and I was working two part-times jobs. The distance between these jobs was more than eighty miles, and I found myself exhausted running between these two jobs. One night, I had a dream about two rings. In the dream, I was getting married and for some reason, the ring was on the wrong hand and kept falling off my finger. This happened twice! After waking up, I was confused about the details of this dream and asked God about the meaning. When the meaning was revealed, the rings symbolized the job. The ring falling off twice and being located on the wrong hand symbolized the fact that the two jobs I was working were not the right fit for me. When I found out what the dream meant, I left both part-time jobs and trusted God to give me one full-time job and He did!!

Another time, God showed me the end of a relationship. In the dream, the young man I had dated for quite a while, turned his back to me and walked away. I called him, however, he did not respond. This dream came true that same year. Over the years God has continued to give me dreams that warn me of danger and situations to avoid.

The longer I walked with God, the more my relationship with Him grew. Of course, this is the way it was supposed to be I was learning how to recognize God's voice and how to distinguish the difference between His voice and my voice.

Passion, Purpose and Society

People often ask me, "Why don't you have kids?" I tell them it is because I am busy building a business brand! My brand is my baby! It's like a plant. For a plant to grow strong, one must water, feed, and nurture it. I nurture and feed my brand with love, hard work, and new ideas.

I am in no rush to have kids. I feel like I am right where I am supposed to be. No two lives are the same. Everything happens in its own time. There is a time to laugh, a time to live, a time to love, and a time to have kids!

In my earlier 20's, I yearned for the traditional life. I wanted to have three children, the house with the white picket fence, and a dog. None of that materialized for me. So, I decided to focus on something I could control and that was my career. I began creating a business out of a passion I had for planning events. With my new business, I knew I was starting something amazing, embarking on my own entrepreneurial journey and building a legacy.

15

THE VISION

Patrick Love

The Birth of a BRAND

In July 2006, one of my aunts asked me to help her plan a Unity Celebration. She and her husband recently had gotten married; however, they did not have a wedding reception. Because they were blending their two families, they decided a Unity Celebration would be a wonderful event.

My aunt and her husband lived two and a half hours away from where I lived. For hours, we conducted our business by phone. At the same time, I was communicating with vendors, finding party favors, and organizing the program.

I had no idea so much work went into planning and coordinating an event.

When my aunt asked me to tell her how much I charged, I told her that I would plan the event for free. This was my first event, and I didn't know what to charge people for my services. Despite what I said, my aunt paid me. I was grateful. This experience allowed me to see that event planning was something I enjoyed doing and something I would do it for free! After this event, I thought about the possibility of turning event planning into a profitable business. With that thought in mind, I began to search for a business name.

On August 11, 2006, my aunt and her husband's Unity Celebration took place at the Princess Anne Civic Center, in Princess Anne, MD. It was a huge success! The bride and groom were totally satisfied with everything I had done! I was very pleased myself!

What's in a Name?

I named my business **Events by Stephanie**. I had business cards and brochures printed. The brochures showed the services I offered and the prices. After some time, I thought that it was time to take my business to the next level. I had used the name, **Events by Stephanie,** from 2006 to the beginning of 2012. During that time, I planned six events while still working my regular full-time job.

When I tried to purchase the original domain name for my business website, **www.eventsbystephanie.com** was already being used by someone. Because I didn't' want any other ending to my website except **.com,** I researched the domain name, **www. stephaniewhiteevents.com**. No one had claimed that name. That was it! My new business name! I loved the sound of **Stephanie White Events**. As opposed to **Events by Stephanie,** this new name seemed to just roll off my tongue! The sound had a richness to it! I purchased the domain name and registered my business name with the State of Maryland, in 2012.

In 2013, I placed my first ad in **Premier Bride Magazine,** a well-known publication circulated in Maryland, Washington, DC, Northern Virginia, and Delaware. Since that time, I have advertised with them twice each year for the last 5 years. This has helped me gain more creditability as a planner and increased my visibility.

To protect both my business and myself, in 2016, **Stephanie White Events** became a limited liability company. My new business cards now read: **Stephanie White Events, LLC.** I was serious about professionally conducting my affairs.

Advertisement: The Key to Business Success

James 2:26 reminds us that "faith without works is dead." I had faith in the ideas God revealed to me for my business, and I knew I had to work if those ideas were going to bear fruit.

As an entrepreneur, I attended bridal shows and networking events in the Washington Metropolitan area.

I met a diverse group of people, including new business owners. The more people I met, the more excited I became about my event planning business.

I knew I had to create a plan to make my business stand out, to make it visible. I started with brochures. Then, I developed a website because revamping my marketing strategy was important. What may have worked at one time may not necessarily continue to be effective.

Although I was willing to work hard, I didn't have a clear plan for my business. All I knew was I liked planning events, and I had a passion for planning events. I had to learn there were two sides to this business, a creative side and a business side. To be successful, I had to master both aspects of event planning.

Along the way, I learned a few lessons the hard way. When I first started planning events, I was so excited about getting clients that I would begin planning and researching for the client's event without even a contract or deposit in place. Sometimes, the client would decide to go another route and not use my services. All the work I had begun to do was for nothing!

Another lesson I learned related to price-setting. If I offered identical services to two people who lived in different areas, one of those people might find the price I charged to be too high. After hearing that a few times, I decided where I would and where I would not seek clients because a worker is worthy of her wages. In addition, I decided to only work with clients who made a deposit.

16

OPPORTUNITIES

Pet Shop Boys

Creating My Own Opportunities

At a time when I was unemployed and looking for creative ways to market my business, a friend who owned a photography business suggested an idea which turned into a tremendous boost for my business. She said, "You enjoy conducting workshops and you enjoy planning weddings. Why don't you combine the two and offer brides and grooms a Bridal Education Workshop? You could help the couple prepare for their upcoming wedding." Immediately, my mental wheels began to turn! I could bring in my wedding industry vendors who could talk with the brides and grooms about what they should know prior to selecting their wedding vendors, and I could speak about the importance of having and hiring a Wedding Planner. These ideas sound great to me!

On January 27, 2013, I produced my first Bridal Education Workshop! It was a success, and the attendees were appreciative of the information they received. At the end of the show, I asked the attendees to complete a survey in which they told what they enjoyed and what they would like to see during the next show. Everyone wanted to see wedding gowns!

In 2016, at my 3rd bridal workshop, I was finally able to bring in a wedding gown vendor and added the Wedding Gown Fashion Show portion to the Education Workshop. I also changed the name of the show to SPRING WEDDING EXTRAVAGANZA BRIDAL EXPO & FASHION SHOW! With this new show name came a new event website for the show, **www.springweddingextravaganza.com**. This website provides updates on upcoming shows, information on our past shows, the vendors, and models for our current show, and other pertinent information.

Relationship building is important in any business, and I am very grateful for the relationships I have with major bridal companies, both locally and nationally. In 2016, Lefty's Bridal & Boutique partnered with me to bring wedding gowns to my bridal show! They were the first bridal gown boutique to work with me in my show.

In 2017, I was able to get David's Bridal onboard to support my March 2017 show which took place at the Double-Tree Hotel, in Silver Spring, MD. This was a bigger show for me and a huge accomplishment because David's Bridal is a worldwide wedding gown distributor. This event also marked my 1st partnership with a major hotel for a bridal expo and bridal fashion show that I produced.

The March 2017 show featured more than twenty models. David's Bridal provided wedding, evening, and bridesmaids gowns. Blank Label Menswear of Washington, DC, provided the clothing for the male models. Additional gowns were provided by the Lamaj Company based in Miami, Florida. The owner of the company attended the event and debuted his very first wedding gown collection, "I DO." This Spring Wedding Extravaganza Bridal Fashion Show was beyond amazing!

In 2013, I decided to organize "A Night to Remember Fundraiser Gala" to honor the memory of my sister Brittany. I contacted the Kennedy Krieger Institute, in Baltimore, where Brittany had been a patient after the 1987 car accident and expressed my desire to raise money for their Brain Injury Unit. My idea was overwhelming accepted by the hospital.

The gala took place in September 2014, at the Sheraton Hotel, in downtown Silver Spring, MD. It was a fabulous, formal affair! Tuxedos and gowns! If I say so myself, my royal blue gown from Lefty's Bridal was gorgeous!

Many friends and family members attended the gala that evening. The doctors from the Brain Injury Unit brought their spouses. Mrs. Downtown Baltimore was the Mistress of Ceremonies, and everyone had an exceptionally enjoyable time. They danced, ate, laughed, and had a ball!

I did not spare any expense for this event. We had a Jazz Band, photo booth, professional photographers, food, DJ, event lighting, and a red carpet!

Money was raised for the Brain Injury Unit through online donations, ticket sales, and the silent auction at the event which offered some wonderful items on which the guests bid: a Signed NFL football from the Baltimore Ravens Football team, tickets for WBLA's show, **The Talk**, Pandora Jewelry from Smyth's Jeweler, and items from Men's Wearhouse. The Men's Wearhouse also offered a discount to the men who had rented their tuxedo or suit from them for my event.

The theme was "A Night to Remember" and, indeed, it was a night to remember. Long after the event ended, I received compliments. In my heart, I knew I would plan a future gala to benefit the Kennedy Krieger Institute's Brain Injury Unit and to honor the memory of my sister, Brittany.

Over the years I continued to develop more marketing avenues for my business. One interesting marketing technique I began to utilize was sponsoring opportunities for other company's shows. The first show I assisted in sponsoring was TASTE OF THE RUNWAY WASHINGTON DC, in Summer 2016. The producer of this show had done several other shows in New York, Philadelphia, Atlanta, and other major cities. It was an honor to work with someone who knew the business so well!

My role as a Sponsor for this show was to create THE BRIDAL SUITE and to handle the Bridal Fashion Show segment of the Fashion show. I contacted my major vendors and my new wedding gown vendors for this creation. I was able to get Cherry Blossom Bridal, located in Washington, DC, to participate as a vendor for the bridal suite and as a wedding gown provider for the bridal fashion segment. I was able to get some of the models who were already participating in the show to model the gowns!

This project allowed me to be as creative as I wanted to be! This type of freedom was awesome! With the help of my contacts, I was able to create a marvelous bridal suite which highlighted many vendors that the newly engaged couples would need in the planning of their wedding. To add to the excitement of the bridal suite, the couples saw an array of beautiful wedding gowns.

By working on this show, the door to the Fashion Show Industry was opened for me. I met models, designers, modeling agency managers, runway coaches, chefs, and other key players. Mostly importantly, I gained some new friends who have become very dear to me. I even had some fun and the opportunity to meet and take photos with Comedian Rodney Perry and Gizelle Bryant, star of **The Real Housewives of Potomac.**

Being a sponsor for this show helped expand my business. It opened doors to a world beyond my wildest dreams.

Television and Radio: New Marketing Avenues

In 2016, a friend who worked for News Channel 8, WJLA in Washington, DC, was instrumental in securing a guest-spot for me on **Let's Talk Live** with host, Julie Wright.

When this opportunity was presented to me, I had to make a quick decision to accept or decline the invitation because the weekend before the Monday morning show, I was going to be in New Orleans for the Total Life Changes Awards, an event associated with another business venture I was pursuing. I didn't know if I would arrive back home in time to appear on Monday's show. I decided this was an opportunity I did not want to miss! I was used to taking risk and handling pressure. I could do this, and I did!

Without flight delays from New Orleans, I arrived home on Sunday evening and arrived early at the studio that Monday morning. I was nervous! Julie Wright was a wonderful interviewer, and her calmness made me calm. During the show, I talked about my upcoming bridal show event and wedding invitation etiquette. For this to have been my first time on television, I think I did a great job. At least, everyone who saw the interview said that I did a great job.

To market my March 5, 2017 Spring Wedding Extravaganza, which was a huge undertaking, the pressure was on to generate massive ticket sales. I had partnered with a nationally-known hotel, and I needed to step up my marketing game. So not only did I do television this time, I also did radio.

I had several commercials read on 97.1 WASH FM and posted via their IHEART Radio APP and website a few days before my event. I had never done radio like this before, so this was new and exciting. This radio station reached a diverse audience in the Washington Metropolitan area; this was a great boost for advertising my upcoming show.

Radio was exciting, but what was even more thrilling was the Mini Bridal Fashion Show I coordinated and presented on one of Washington, DC's television stations, WUSA, Channel 9. Again, this opportunity came through someone whom I had met while planning one of my bridal shows. A model who had participated in one of the shows had a connection at WUSA. She arranged for me to be a guest on the show, **Great Day Washington.**

Oh my! Presenting a Mini-fashion Show on television meant I needed models, garments, make-up, and something to wear! Last year, when I appeared on television, I didn't have the opportunity to get my make-up professionally done for the show. This year, I wanted to make sure I got the works!

In preparation for the Mini Bridal Fashion Show, I asked three vendors to provide the garments for the models. The menswear vendor, Blank Label, provided two suits for the men. David's Bridal provided two wedding gowns and the Lamai Company shipped one of their newly designed gowns from their "I DO" collection.

I prayed to God through this whole process! I felt if it were meant to be, it would be! Evidently, it was meant to be because, with hard work and determination, everything came together for this show, in February 2017.

The Mini Bridal Fashion Show participants were three female models and two male models. A wonderful friend who is a make-up artist granted my wish and arrived to do my make-up.

Preparing for **Great Day Washington** took a lot of time, energy, and patience. So many emails and phone calls! The finished product, however, was amazing! The show was more than I imagined it would be. What a marvelous opportunity to showcase **Stephanie White Events!**

You Mean the World to Me

When I listen to Toni Braxton's Song, "You Mean the World to Me," I can't help but to think about God who has given me so many opportunities to experience success with my business. Freedom, creativity, abundance, joy, love, happiness, fulfillment, purpose, destiny, passion, and legacy are the words I use to describe my business and this entrepreneurial journey. I view my business as my gift to the world. God gave me a thought, and I turned it into a business. Everything I have done, I have done only because God has allowed me to create and to execute! I look forward to more of what God has in store for me and my business in the future!

17

JOY AND PAIN
Rob Base & DJ EZ Rock

A Joyful Place

Whether it's music, my family, my church family or my business, I like to surround myself with things that bring me joy because there were so many days when I had no joy.

I remember the times when I was unemployed. I would sit alone in my apartment and ask God about the future of my life. During those times, I would write a lot in my journal and talk to Aunt B who didn't mind sharing stories from her own life. She was honest about the mistakes she had made and the lessons she learned. She didn't want to see me make some of the same mistakes. She and I would often refer to the book I called my "Woman Thou Art Loosed Bible." The real title was the **Holy Bible: Woman Thou Art Loosed!,** edited by Bishop T. D. Jakes. My goodness! This book has gotten a girl through many a difficult day. The stories and essays about women in this Bible helped recharge my soul. My Aunt B and I would talk for hours, using this Bible to give me some guidance. I look back on those days and I thank God for those teaching moments with Aunt B.

I believe purpose, passion, and joy go hand in hand. I believe your purpose can be many things in this life, but your passion is that one thing which wakes you up in the morning, that thing you would do for free, and that thing which makes your heart smile. I generally believe people feel joy and excitement when they have a specific direction in which they are heading in life. When people have purpose, it makes them feel useful.

Throughout my life, God has shown me so much favor to the point where I sometimes felt I was not deserving of His blessings. Sometimes, I had to ask the Lord, "IS THIS MY LIFE I AM LIVING, God?" Why do I feel the need to question my life and all God has blessed me with? I think, when you are used to situations not going your way, it is surprising when things begin to happen for you.

Whenever something good happened in my life, I always feared something bad was right behind it. Instead of enjoying what God had blessed me with, I allowed fear to snatch the joy I should have been experiencing. What this did was take away my joy of enjoying this great thing with which God had blessed me. It got to the point where I wouldn't get too excited about anything. I guess I thought the blow wouldn't be too hard when something bad happened, if I didn't get too excited about the good! Was I conditioned to think that something bad was going to happen? So many unpleasant situations had occurred in my life, I didn't know how I would take it if another bad thing happened. Can you imagine the emotional tug-of-war going in my head?

As life has gone on, I have learned to control my emotions. I am still a work in progress; however, I am not where I used to be. Joy is a rare commodity, and I try to maintain as much of it as I can.

PART II

THE

JOURNEY

CONTINUES

18

YOU OUGHTA KNOW

IAlanis Morissette

Anger Misplaced

Misplaced anger has a way of getting in the way of progress. Even though I was progressing through life, making what I call" Boss Lady" moves with my company, I still had some things with which I had not dealt with. To be honest with you, I had no idea that, for my life to progress in a positive way even more than it had already done, I had to deal with the areas that were holding me in uncomfortable emotional positions. This discomfort had to do with my relationship with my father, LT.

I was angry with my father because of the years he had not done right by Brittany and me. We became wards of the state because he didn't do what a father should have done. I assumed he felt his duties as a father ended once we were placed in the care of someone else. Regardless of how he might have felt, I still needed and wanted my father. I needed to feel connected to my only living parent. I was angry with my father because he wouldn't be what I wanted him to be. Because of this, I built high emotional walls to prevent being hurt again the way I had been hurt by my father.

Now, don't get me wrong. I am thankful I have my father because there are a lot of people who don't know their father. Though my father was oftentimes not physically present, I stayed connected to him through his family which is my family. Then, if for some reason, his family lost contact with him. All I had to do to find my dad was go to the town of Princess Anne and ask anyone on the street or at the corner store, "Have you seen LT?" Automatically, they would say that they had seen him because my dad knew a lot of people and a lot of people knew him.

19

EVERY MAN SHOULD KNOW
Harry Connick, Jr.

He is Born

To truly understand my dad, you must know his background. As mentioned earlier, born in 1956, my father came from a very large family of twenty siblings. He was one of the younger siblings. His mother was a stay-at-home mom for a while. Then, she became employed outside of the home. My dad's father graduated from Seminary School and was a local preacher who traveled from church to church. I've been told that my grandfather raised chickens, hogs, ducks and geese to take care of his family. He had a big garden where he grew potatoes, sweet potatoes, lima beans, cabbages, tomatoes, cucumbers and other vegetables.

Was My Dad Ready?

Traditionally, years ago, when you became an adult, you married and started a family. The husband got a job and took care of the financial needs of the family, and the wife cooked, cleaned and took care of the children. Getting married was the normal thing people did. Was everyone ready for that kind of commitment?

When my dad married my mom in 1978, he was 21 and getting ready to join the service. Was my dad ready for everything that came along with being a husband? Was he ready to be a father or was he still too young to grasp the knowledge of what it takes to be responsible and take care of a family? Was my father a man on the outside, but a child on the inside! Was he a man-child? Yes, it is true that women mature faster than men on so many different levels. So, to put it gently, I don't think my dad was ready for this responsibility at such a young age.

Prior to the death of my mother and older sister, I was unaware of any unhappiness which may have existed between my parents. I was a child and most of the time, parents try to hide things from their kids. I remember seeing my mother upset at times, but I didn't quite know why. I remember one day the police came to our home. My mother stood outside, talking to the police. Inside of the house, standing at the door, my father was smiling. I thought it was a game my father was playing. I later learned my father had locked my mother out of the house and she had called the police.

I try to mentally put myself in my mother's shoes and try to imagine what she was feeling at this time in her life. I also try to mentally put myself in my father's shoes and get a feel for where his head was during this time. Was my mother alone in this fight to build a life for her girls or was my father somewhere in the background fighting the same fight? I don't know. Maybe, my father was just very immature and selfish at the time.

What I have learned is people react differently to life's situations. Some pray while others drink. Some look for the positive in life, while others act crazy and harm others. People can be physically abusive towards their spouse or partners, and they can be mentally abusive as well.

20

ALL YOU NEVER SAY

Birdy

Physically Present, Mentally Gone

Is it possible to be somewhere mentally and not there physically? Maybe or maybe not, but it is possible to be somewhere physically and not be there mentally. I believe this was my father. Yes, he was there physically for the day to day activities. If you asked him a question, he would answer. There were times; however, when he wasn't there mentally. Would you be mentally there if your life had been turned upside down in an instant? My father was in a mental fog after the death of my mother and my sister. What had to be harder than a father having to identify the body of his wife and the body of his daughter? I believe my father didn't know whether he was coming or going.

The Mask My Father Wore

My father used many things to mask the pain and guilt he was feeling, including substances his body didn't need. Some people believe it is better to be under the influence of a substance as opposed to being sober and dealing with the reality of life. You can only hide for so long. I believe my father wore a mask for years. The mask changed overtime. My father went from using substances to mask his pain to hiding behind lies. I guess a lie sometimes sounds better than the truth! I got to a place in my life where I didn't believe a lot of what my father told me. At the time he wasn't telling the truth, I never let him know I didn't believe him. My father began to build a reputation for stretching the truth about matters which needed no truth-stretching. At this point in my life, I was grown and didn't need my father in the way I needed him when I was a child. Whether he told the truth or not, it didn't matter to me.

In 2017, my father let down his guard and put away his masks. He never received the therapy he needed to help him cope with the grief of losing my mother and sister. It would have been good for him to have spoken with someone who specialized in counseling widowers and grieving parents. Instead, my father tried to navigate through his pain by himself. This can be a very dangerous thing to do. I think counseling would have helped my father move beyond the walls he put up to mask his hurt and guilt.

The Gifts My Father Gave

Regardless of what my father couldn't do for me, I am grateful for what he did do for me. My father gave me life. Yes, I know it was a collaborative effort between him and my mother. But yes! He gave me life. Although I don't have my maternal sisters, my father is responsible for the four paternal sisters I have.

When my mother was alive, she and my dad tried to give us girls a good life. They provided a home for us; this was love. Even after the accident, my father provided a home for us and made sure Brittany and I went to school. He tried to create some childhood memories for us as well until Social Services came and took us away.

Another gift my father gave to me is smarts! He is extremely skilled in math. As a child, I had a lot of issues with math and my father used to sit at the kitchen table and work math problems with me. We did this every night, and I hated it! My father was patient with me and took his time going over all the problems with me. Then, he would have me work on them. Sometimes, I could not grasp the concept. He never gave up trying to teach me.

I know my father's likes, dislikes, favorite foods, and favorite music. I cannot imagine what it would be like going through life and never having known my father. I have come to realize his very existence is a gift.

21

YOU LEARN

Alanis Morissette

Forgive and Live!

For many years, my relationship with my father resembled a roller-coaster ride. Then, a few years ago, our relationship stabilized for the better.

The first breakthrough occurred when I went to visit my father who was incarcerated for the umpteenth time for non-payment of child support. Based on what I had been told, this was the only crime for which my dad had ever been detained in jail. This time, he reached out to me and asked me to put money in his commissary account. My first reaction was anger. Within myself, I said, "NO."

A day or two later, I had a dream in which God showed me a glimpse of my future life. During that sneak-preview, I was miserable and bitter because I had not forgiven my father. After this dream, though I didn't want to go, I knew I had to go and see my dad.

Before I made the trip, I settled another issue with which I had been wrestling. I knew my father did not have an insurance policy, and if he died, the family would look to me to bury him. Buying that policy would be another expense, and I already had enough expenses. Then, I realized the purchasing of a policy would free me from the awful and dreadful situation of having to raise money or deplete my savings account to give my father a proper burial. With that thought in mind, I moved forward and purchased the life insurance policy.

Once I arrived at the detention center, I had to leave my belongings with the guard. I was escorted into a room where a glass wall separated the guests from inmates. When my dad entered the room, he and I communicated by phone. My father said that he was surprised to see me, and that I was the last person he thought he would see. We didn't have much time to talk. I had to get right to what I had come to do. After we asked about each other's welfare, I began to tell my dad that I forgave him for everything he did and didn't do for me while I was young. I told my dad that I loved him. That was the gist of our conversation. Before I left the detention center that day, I put money in my father's commissary account. Though my visit to see my father wasn't easy that day, I did what I had to do.

Forgiveness was the only way! I had to forgive my father for what he had not done for my sister and me. I had to forgive my father for how he treated us as kids. I had to forgive him for not giving me the attention I desperately needed. I had to forgive my father for what he couldn't give. Was I looking for something from my father that he just simply couldn't give? Did my dad give us everything he had to give and there was nothing left? I had to forgive! Forgiving my father was the only way I could be free! Forgiveness was not only for my dad, but for me as well. No, this process did not happen overnight. In my heart, I had to forgive my father again and again and again! When I forgave my dad, I felt a freedom that could not be explained. It was like the chains were broken, and I was free. Of course, I had moments when past negative memories would creep into my head, and the process of forgiving my father would began anew.

The Breakthrough We Needed

Six days after my 35th birthday, my father and I met for lunch. On the way to the restaurant, I shared some music I knew he would enjoy! Some of the songs were his favorite songs.

As we sat and ate, my father showed a side of himself I had never seen. He admitted to things he once had denied and acknowledged mistakes he had made in life. It was as if he exposed the essence of his soul. I saw the real man who was my father. We talked adult to adult, with sincerity.

I shared what was happening in my life, and he shared what was happening in his life. There was a feeling of easiness between us. The tension which had existed between us in the past had disappeared. I showed him photos of some of my client's events, and we talked about his business as well. After we finished our lunch, my dad paid the bill and left the tip! I was impressed!

On the way back to my dad's home, I played some Go-Go music for my dad. I even played one of my dad's favorite songs, "Can You Get It" by Mandrill. While that song played, my father talked about his teenage years when he and my uncle listened to this song, while my aunts got ready to go to the club. This song took him back to a time when things were simple. He related how, throughout his life, people judged him. "All I tried to do was live my life," he said. He even spoke about his so-called friends who turned out to not be his friends at all.

At that moment, how I looked at my father suddenly changed. I saw my father as someone who had made some mistakes, yet others had tried to continue to make him pay for those mistakes. I saw a man who had been mentally beaten and who had been constantly judged. This man, my father, had hid behind lies and wore masks which only temporarily fixed how he felt. I saw a man who needed help, but didn't know who to trust and how to ask for help. I began to feel compassion for my father. I felt his pain. When I looked into his eyes, I felt the need to protect him; his life had been hard.

My advice to my dad was to learn who was for him and who was against him. I also encouraged him to forgive himself for past mistakes. He said that he had forgiven himself.

At the end of the day, all I want is the best for my father. I want him to live out the remainder of his days in a state of peace and contentment. I love my dad, and I try to tell him that I love him often as I can!

Like me, my dad has an entrepreneurial spirit. He started a handy man/repair business for which I made him business cards. Fixing things is his passion, and he is good at what he does. Past customers have nothing but great things to say about my father and the work he does. I am thankful my father has found his niche in life.

22

GOD'S FAVOR
Donald Lawrence and The
Tri City Singers

Favor

When I review my life, I can clearly see God's favor. For one thing, He didn't allow me to become a "basket-case" despite the tragedy which affected my life. I know it was God who moved on the hearts of my aunt and uncle to adopt me. Through their kindness, I received free college and owed a mere $800.00 in school loans when I graduated. That loan was paid in less than six months! It was God's plan for me to move to the Washington, DC Metropolitan area two months after I graduated from undergraduate school. This move set in motion the biggest successes in my event planning business.

God showed me unlimited favor in the two and a half year I was unemployed. I was able to get the things I needed and take care of my bills. Those lean years taught me to recognize the faithfulness of God, and I never failed to thank Him for His blessings. During my unemployment, I didn't understand what was happening in my life. Little did I know that through the favor of God, he was allowing me to rest and prepare for big things ahead!

To Whom Much is Given, Much is Required

After many good jobs and many great opportunities, God placed me in the position where I was able to give back to others. I facilitated a Saturday morning workshop with some local school children wherein I taught them how to set a proper table. At my church, I taught a social media class for the youth. They learned what was appropriate to post on their social media sites and what was not appropriate to post.

I even did a few pro bono events. Giving back made me feel good inside because when you help others, you also help yourself in the process. What I've come to realize is we are not put on this earth for self; we are here to serve others. Everything we go through, we go through to help others. It doesn't always feel good in the beginning, but once you get on the other side of that thing or situation, you can help someone else through the same situation. It all equates to giving back!

When I was 10, I spent a night in a shelter because there were serious problems at home. I never stopped thinking about the people who lived in those shelters every day; they had no home.

In 2012, I begin volunteering at Sarah's House, a shelter whose residents included entire families. During my time of service, I facilitated two workshops: Taking Better Care of Self and Money Management. I also organized toy drives and other drives to collect items needed by the residents of the shelter. Once, I even coordinated a Thanksgiving game day with the youth from my church and the youth at Sarah's house. The youth from my church played and sang with the kids at the shelter, and the adults got involved as well. The youth from my church even donated items to the shelter. They did a wonderful job! It was a joy to see the grateful families.

23

PIECES OF ME

Ledisi

A Flower Begins to Blossom

When a baby is born, they know nothing of this world. They are innocent. They have a clean slate. Their hearts only know the love of their mother and father. They have no preconceived knowledge about this world and what good and bad exist in this world. Babies smile when they are happy, cry when they are sad, hungry, need to be changed, or have a stomach ache. They love you with the purest love.

Then, life begins to happen. The good, bad, ugly, unpleasant, joy, pain, sorrow, sadness and all the above. Add to those things, everything we are taught: morals values, what feelings to have, what feelings not to have, how a girl should act, how a boy should act, what one should wear, and what one shouldn't wear. The layers of life pile on, one by one.

That once pure baby is now a teenager who has been bullied, chastised, hurt, left behind, and conditioned to think that life is all about survival, success, and no happiness. The teenager grows into an adult who has taken on the values once instilled in her. Not happy, the adult now wears rejection on her face and sadness in her eyes. She has taken on the persona of not one person but, many people. This adult never learned how to be an individual and runs from the person God has made her to be. One day, she doesn't know herself. The layers which have been loaded and reloaded onto her for many years have now turned the purest person into a dysfunctional and confused adult! She is an adult who no longer knows her own way, but only the way of this world. She is an adult who is asleep. I was that person! I was asleep and didn't even know it.

What would have become of me had I been groomed for a life of greatness and passion? I might have known more joy than sorrow, been more open to meet new people, and been more open to try new things. Instead, I created walls to protect me from harm and to protect my feelings. Soon, those walls kept me from feeling anything at all.

These walls were like layers of an onion. Each layer needed to be pulled back, piece by piece. Those layers were symbolic of layers of sadness, rejection, other people's opinions, other people's thoughts, and other people's ways of life.

To blossom into all that God made me to be, I first needed to heal past hurts, disappointments, and pain. Healing is a very important process in one's life. Healing needs to take place for one to go to the next level or levels that God has for them in life. You can't expect to move forward in life with baggage from your past; it weighs you down and blocks your blessings. When the healing is complete, your true essence of who you are will be revealed.

This AUTHENIC person God has made is finally ready to be revealed to the world! This world is waiting for us to put away the COUNTERFEIT TO REVEAL THE AUTHENIC SELF! THE TRUE SELF!

24

POCKETFUL OF SUNSHINE
Natasha Bedingfield

AWAKE! Journey to a NEW Self-Discovery

In the spring of 2015, I began to feel unusually different. I yearned to commune with nature. The trees and the wind had an unexplainable influence on me! It was peaceful. I would sit outside for long periods of time, looking at the sky. Even watching the birds was enjoyable. I liked being outside more than I liked being inside with people. Even breathing the air was refreshing! Being close to nature was like being closer to God.

A shift was taking place within me: a shift in my thoughts and a shift in my focus. I was intrigued about this inner change. I wanted to know what was happening with me and if other people experienced the same thing I was experiencing. What was it? Who could I tell? Who would understand what I was experiencing?

As these unusual feelings continued, I noticed I could not tolerate anything superficial. I only related to relationships and friendships which were authentic. I refused to invest in shallow relationships which could not grow beyond their current state. There was going to be no higher level because light and dark cannot exist in the same space.

This shift I experienced also caused me to be hypersensitive. My emotions, imagination, and inspiration were heightened. I guarded my energy and allowed only positive energy in my space. Not only did I guard against people with negative energy, I guarded what my eyes saw and what my ears heard. Positive energy was the only energy with which I wanted to interact.

When my unusual feelings did not subside, I knew it was time to conduct some research. My reading led me to the term, *spiritual awakening.* The more I read, the more I identified with my experiences. I was on a journey! A Spiritual Awakening!

The **Urban Dictionary** defines *spiritual awakening* as a shift in consciousness, an apperception of reality which had been previously unrealized. Apperception is how your mind puts new information in context. For example, you get a perception of a chair through the eyes, but apperception is how your mind relates that chair to chairs you have seen before.

To be **awake** is to be aware of and actively attentive to important facts and issues. I believe **awake** can also apply to someone who is aware of their surroundings, their spiritual self, their purpose, and the true essence of who they are as a person.

In the very beginning of this journey, there was no one I felt I could talk to about what I was experiencing. I wasn't sure who was awake and who was asleep! Would people think I was crazy? I struggled to make sense of this new world I was discovering. These new thoughts and feelings were very exciting because it was as if I were rediscovering a new world. This world had always been there; however, it had been buried under layers of stuff I no longer needed.

Finally! I was myself! I felt like a kid, walking this earth for the first time. It was as if loads and loads of stuff just began to fall off me and what was left was a child-like spirit within me! I began to love to laugh, enjoy life, and have a good time. I had hidden this side of myself for far too long! Although I feel I always have been gentle and kind, I became gentler and kinder to others. Now, don't misunderstand me, I still let it be known whenever something displeased me. For example, if someone tried to belittle me, they soon learned I was not going to tolerate that behavior because it was unacceptable. I was loving myself and this new journey; I was not about to go in reverse. No more layers!

Another part of my spiritual awakening was the increase in synchronicities or simultaneous occurrences. Usually, these occurrences were number-related. I don't gamble in any form (lotteries, etc.); therefore, I didn't understand why I continued to see the same numbers. Lottery players probably would have been excited and played the occurring number/numbers. I never connected to the numbers in that sense. I only wanted to know the meaning of the reoccurring numbers.

For example, the numbers 5 and 821 were the two numbers I constantly saw. The number, 821, was significant to me because this number represents my birthday. I was born in the eighth month and the 21st day. I saw these numbers everywhere! I saw them on license plates, clocks, and on the television. In time, I believed whenever I observed the reoccurrence of numbers, one of two things was happening. I either was on the right path and had to keep moving or opportunities were coming my way and I had to be prepared.

On this journey, I desired to change my diet. I became more aware of what I put in my mouth. Initially, I drastically decreased my intake of beef, chicken, and turkey. Then, I stopped eating those foods and consumed only seafood. Still, there are more changes to come as I become more conscious of a healthy-lifestyle.

A crucial part of spiritual awakening is creating new belief systems. There was a time when I wanted lots of material things. Now, I want more freedom and less stuff. Clutter and I don't mix well anymore! Less is more!

I was blessed to purchase a new home in 2016, and in my new space, I have taken on this notion of less is more! I want my home to be elegant, enjoyable, and beautiful, but not cluttered. I feel more at ease when my home is neat and not full of stuff.

As I became more awake, I suddenly desired a change in employment. I have been working the same job for several years, and I thought I was overdue for something different. Yes, I have my business, but I also work a full-time job. I What is it that God will have me do next? I don't want to go through life, struggling and wondering how I can live my most fulfilled life and take care of my responsibilities at the same time. I am ready for a change, and I am open to whatever that looks like. What I have learned about being spiritually awake is that when you are open to possibilities, new things come your way.

At home, I am blessed to have a quiet environment where I can talk to God. It's wonderful to have times when I can freely speak aloud and there's no one present to look at me like I'm crazy because I am talking to someone whom they can't see. My conversations with God have increased. Several times a day, I thank my God for all His blessings. I talk to God about my heart's desires, my happiness, and unhappiness. I spend time talking with God about my next move and what decisions I should make. I try to include God in every decision I make; however, there are times when I am guilty of not seeking God's guidance as to what He would have me to do and what I can do for Him.

Sometimes, in my communication with God, I miss the mark! I am a work in progress, and God continues His work in me.

Let's Straighten This Out

Before I move forward, I want to clarify something. Some of the ideas I have expressed are my beliefs; they do not have to accepted by anyone else. Later, I will talk about the Law of Attraction, and that concept might not be a concept you believe. It is, however, a concept I believe. At one time, I was very rigid in my thoughts and would never have considered exploring the Law of Attraction. My belief system changed, and I am not that same rigid individual. Sometimes, *rigid* means *judgmental*. I have been guilty of judging when I didn't understand someone else's thinking. I believe we all are prone to judge when we don't understand someone's path or journey. Being judgmental lessens when we agree we all are in this world together trying to make something out of this thing called LIFE.

I still am a Christian, and I still believe in the Father, the Son and the Holy Ghost. I just try to lead with love more than anything else. God is love and we should treat others with love, regardless of their belief system. Let us lead with love!

25

DANGER ZONE

Kenny Loggins

33-Year- Old: Mid-life Crisis

For most of my life, I have tried to do the right thing. Before making decisions, I think and oftentimes, overthink what to do. This was not the case in June 2015, during the beginning stages of my spiritual awakening. I was excited about my new-found courage and freedom! In one area of my life, however, there was new-found dumbness! Based on my feelings as opposed to my usual good, sound thinking, I made a poor decision. Instead of going right, I went left. I allowed myself to get involved with a man who was attached to someone else! It started with a kiss which sparked feelings which I thought were "long dead" in me. I would have never thought this would have happened in a million years!

As soon as he kissed me, I knew it was wrong! Wrong! Wrong! I turned and ran from him. In that moment, I knew what had happened shouldn't have happened. This kiss frightened me because I was a person who never allowed a married person to get that close to me. I thought, "You are married. What were you doing? Better yet, what were you thinking?" After several days had passed, I thought more and more about that kiss. I was ashamed to admit I enjoyed it! Days later, he and I had a conversation. I asked him what made him kiss me, and he said that he wanted to end the tension that was between us. This kiss, many weeks later, led to a one-night of passion after we met and had too many drinks at "Happy Hour." It happened only once! Just once! But, once was enough.

I am ashamed to admit we texted each other throughout the remainder of 2015. Since we knew some of the same people, it was only natural a group of us would sometimes get together. I wanted to keep it that way; there was safety in a crowd. I was hooked on him and knew I shouldn't had been. He felt badly about the encounter and thought he might have ruined a friendship we once shared. I admitted to myself that he was not the only one to blame; I was to blame as well. Drunk or not drunk, I had decided to allow my heart to overrule my head.

The time after that one drunken night was an interesting time. I was angry with myself because I couldn't let go of my feelings. Sometimes, men can have affairs and walk away as if nothing ever happened. Females, on the other hand, 'catch feelings." We internalize the experience and can't understand why it meant so little to the man. How could I have "caught feelings?"

In some twist turn of fate, one day I ended up in the same space with his wife. We were like two ships passing in the night. I knew about her, but she knew nothing about me. I was mad with myself! How could I have stooped so low? I felt like I was sneaking around, and I was the only one with these feelings. I could never be in a relationship with this man; yet, I couldn't get him out of my head. What was the matter with me? This was not who I was. I would never have dreamed of doing this to another woman, but I did! This was not the person I wanted to be. I had to awaken from my current state of mind.

When I woke up, I admitted to myself that God made me to be more than a potential "side piece." This communicating with this married man was going nowhere because regardless of what he either said or didn't say about his marriage, he was where he wanted to be. After much thought and many questions, I realized I didn't want him. I was on a completely different path in life, and I needed to stay on that path!

When I woke up from this "bad dream," I knew it was time for Stephanie to move on with her life! I had to discontinue all communication with him and that's exactly what I did! Whenever I saw him, I was polite; however, that was the extent of our communication. I had an agenda, and I was sticking to it!

During this time, I did something else I never thought I would do. I had a few sessions with psychics. I had to understand why I was strongly attracted to a man who could never be my man. It wasn't enough for me to just go through the experience of this situation. I wanted to know why it happened. The psychics told me that there was a strong connection between this man and me. They also mentioned he was someone who wanted to be attached to people who made him look good; he wanted to hang onto their coattails. He depended on the success of others to make him look successful.

Countless times throughout the year when he and I were communicating, I would think about him and suddenly, I would receive a text from him. Have you ever experienced this with a person? This is an example of synchronicity which is defined as simultaneous occurrences and coincidental occurrence of events, especially psychic events that seem related but are not explained by conventional mechanisms of causality.

During this time of researching my new experiences, I discovered the term, twin flame relationship. A twin flame relationship is the most powerful relationship you can experience in this lifetime. A twin flame serves as a mirror for you, a mirror of your own soul issues. Of course, this was all new to me! Meeting your twin flame is like meeting yourself in another person.

When meeting your twin flame, you feel a magnetic pull towards one another and that magnetic pull is what I felt towards my friend during the year we were communicating. I couldn't understand why I felt such a pull towards him. I know it sounds weird but, I can only explain what I experienced. After much research, I concluded, I had met my twin flame!

According to the information I read, in twin flame relationships, you can sense when something is going wrong in your twin flame's life! The funny thing is that during the time I was involved with this man, I experienced a vivid dream which spoke volumes about him and his situations. In the dream, there was immense tension between this man and his current situation. I awoke from that dream and was in shock! Why did I have this dream? I asked God what he was showing me and why he would give me such a dream since He knew how I felt about this person. I knew that this was one of those God-given dreams because I had already experienced many vivid dreams before wherein God warned me about things. I spoke with some of my spiritual and Christian friends about the dream. Of course, I didn't tell them about my intimate involvement with this man. One friend told me to start praying for him and his spouse. After not wanting to pray for them, I decided to be obedient. This was hard for me because I still had feelings for this man. On the other hand, I knew there was a reason for my dream. I also knew God would confirm what He had shown to me.

God sent confirmation about my dream through an acquaintance who knew both this man and his wife. Without any prompting on my part, the acquaintance told me about the conflict happening with the couple and their current situation. This confirmed the turmoil and the content of my dream.

At the end of the day, I decided I deserved better than what I was allowing with this man. I have no ill will against him and I wish him and his family all the best.

With this experience, I had let down walls to experience life in a new way, even if it were only for a moment with the wrong person. For a while, I felt more alive than I had felt in a long time. I know what I did was wrong, and there are consequences to be paid. Good or bad, all actions trigger a reaction.

I believe. in some crazy way, this experience was supposed to be a part of my spiritual awakening. For the first time in my life, my walls came down. I was operating in a zone that was natural to me even if it were unfamiliar. Oh yes, by the way, the synchronicities which connected me with this man ceased when I cut off all communication with him.

26

WEIGHTLESS
Natasha Bedingfield

True to Self

Authenticity is important! It is the state of something or someone being genuine, legitimate, or true. When I began to live my true self, I released old ways of thinking and developed new ways of thinking and living. I embraced certain attributes and characteristics of myself that I once ignored. My fun and playful side began to emerge. I was happy because I no longer felt I had to "dumb-down" that side of my personality which is fun, playful, loves to laugh hysterically, and watch funny movies. I want to shine when I enter a room, and that's alright with me! I am a people- person, and I like to interact with new people. I am a very sensitive person who is much like my grandmother used to be; she "wore her heart on her sleeve." I have been told, that I "wear my heart on my sleeve" as well. I have compassion for others, and sometimes I get caught up in other people's problems. I don't mind crowds. I like to be around like-minded people, and I gravitate towards others who have the same energy I have! Most of the time, I have very high energy which sometimes can be too much for some people.

Have you ever felt like you couldn't be yourself because being yourself was way too much for other people? Well, I once had the experience wherein I felt the need to alter my personality to make other people feel comfortable. I recognized that in some situations, this was acceptable. In other situations, it was not acceptable. Ultimately, I want to be myself and not change to make people comfortable.

As I began to live my authentic self, I began to value myself and my opinions at a much higher level than I ever did in the past. It is funny how life will sometimes make you forget you once had your own mind, your own opinions, your own likes, and dislikes. Now, I have begun to see life through different eyes, new eyes. Things changed the moment I began to embrace who Stephanie was as a person. I truly love who I am and who I've become. I am a hard-working woman who has her own style and her own way of looking at things. I am a woman who is anxious at times when I must make a big decision, but eventually I get back in the game and push forward. I allow fear to challenge me to higher heights! I am a woman who felt extremely lost growing up in a world that was so big and vast. Yes, I am a woman who still misses her mother and two sisters, and yes, I am woman who still, in her 30's, needs to hear her dad say that he is proud of her.

Growing up, I had a time-table for my life. In my 20's, I wanted to be married. Eventually, I wanted three children just like my mother had three children. Now, I still want to get married. Three children? Maybe not!

The timeline I had for my career is moving in the right direction. I am thankful to God and to people whom God placed in my life to guide me. Some of my goals have shifted to my benefit. Some things I didn't know I wanted until later in my career are currently happening. For that, I am grateful.

Regardless of what I have yet to accomplish, I am in a happy space, a space where I am true to myself. If there is something I prefer not to do, I don't do it. Finally, I have reached that place where I no longer live for others; I live for myself. You do arrive at that place in life where you stop being overly concerned about what others think and say. You pay more attention to your thoughts and your feelings. Now, I realize that to get to where I am today and to truly appreciate my progress, I had to go through the pain, suffering, tears and sorrow to come out on the other side. A constant reminder for me is that everything we go through is not necessarily for us, but for others.

This journey to my authentic self has allowed me to loosen up and enjoy the simpler things in life. I love Rock & Instrumental Jazz music. Sometimes, I think I was born in the wrong era because I love 80's movies such as **The Breakfast Club, Coming to America, The Goonies** and the legendary movie, **Purple Rain**, starring the Artist formerly known as Prince. I love old school hip-hop from the 90's era, clothing from the 80's, and dancing from the 70's! I love Donna Summers, Elton John, Aerosmith, Soul Asylum, and John Mellencamp!

I am in a space where I am very comfortable with being me. I love the skin I am in.

Okay, let me not lie. Sometimes, I don't always love this body with the few extra pounds I 've gained but, overall, I love the skin I am in!

Break Every Chain

I believe people only look back to see how far they've come, how much progress they've made, and how to move forward. When I look back, I see things which enslaved me. I see a person on an emotional rollercoaster which was going nowhere fast. Yes, my emotions kept me in bondage. How I felt most days was contingent upon how others received me, responded to me, and interacted with me. My emotions would go up and down. It was a mentally hard place to be. I needed to do some major internal work.

How I felt about my life was affected by society, television, radio, my peers, and my job. I had taken on the persona of not only other people's feelings towards me, but also the world's opinion of what was in style and popular.

Then, the awakening I experienced made me feel worthy and valuable. It was reminisced of a line from "Break Every Chain" by Tasha Cobbs. She says, I hear the chains falling." Suddenly, I was no longer bond! Truly, things happen when they are supposed to happen, not when we want them to happen. God's timing is perfect!

27

I CAN SEE CLEARLY NOW

Johnny Nash

NEW 20/20 VISION

I had been so used to doing what I had been taught for so many years that I didn't know any other way to live. I was like a machine! My schedule every day was the same! I got up five days a week, went to work, went to the gym, came home, got up Saturday morning to run errands, went to bed, got up Sunday morning, went to church, came home and prepared myself for another work week. I followed this same routine for years! It was to the point where I didn't know any other way and I felt stuck. Then, I got tired and made a change. This happened a few times during my life.

With the changes, I made in my routine also came the change I made in myself. I stopped doing things for the sake of doing them, and I stopped being busy for the sake of being busy. Since I started making a life for myself in the Washington DC Metropolitan area, I had become busy and sometimes my busyness was due to trying to appear productive to impress other people. Sometimes, I used my busyness to cover up my loneliness. I don't do that anymore. When you see the error of your ways, you change. This is what I did. Instead of pretending, I dealt with my issues. I put aside my busyness and my loneliness and began to take control of my mental energy. My busyness now has meaning! Life never looked so clear!

Change is about growth. Usually, you know it's time for change when you become restless. This happens when you are no longer satisfied with a thing. Perhaps, in the place where you are, you have learned all you need to learn. Well, that's how I felt about my place of worship. I loved my church but, I felt like I was ready to move on to something new. It has taken me a long time to admit this because going to church was something my family did every Sunday.

At this point in my life, I felt like I had done so much good in my church and maybe it was time for me to move on to something else. I had joined so many ministries to the extend where I was sometimes busy doing church work two or three days a week. I had worked with the singles, the new members, current members, and the youth. I attended conferences, Christmas programs, Easter programs, Men's Day programs, Women's Day programs, Church festivals, etc. I had generously given my time to help others, and I needed to be relieved of the constant hustle and bustle. As I began to slow down, it got to a point where I just wanted to attend church, sit in a pew, hear the Word and go home. I didn't want to do anything else. It was almost like I wanted to be invisible. The people-person I am would not allow that much disconnection with life.

Then, I felt an overwhelming thirst for more knowledge. I wanted more, and I knew more had to be out there. I knew there had to be more to life than what was within the four walls of my church. Was it time for me to move on? Was it time for me to find another church? What did I feel led to do? A friend once told me that you mentally leave a place long before you physically leave a place. This is true for your job, relationships, and for your church. Was I mentally gone from this place, but still there physically? I enjoyed the WORD my pastor preached every Sunday, and I enjoyed the singing by the choirs as well. I, however, didn't feel totally fulfilled any longer at my home church. What was going on with me?

The first time I missed church, I felt so guilty. For as long as I could remember, I had gotten up on Sunday mornings and gone to church. I did this for years! This routine was embedded in me. I knew no other way.

The second time I missed Sunday Church, I really felt guilty. It was as if I could I hear my family saying, "You always go to church first and give thanks to God. Then, you go on with the rest of your day. You plan your day around church." I felt ashamed to let my aunt know I hadn't attended church that day. As time went on, I attended church less and less.

One thing about going to a Mega Church is that you also have the option of watching church service online. Our church had three locations; therefore, we had about four to six opportunities on Sundays to get the word via internet. Most Sundays, I took advantage of one of these opportunities.

Some may ask, "Is she still connected to God?" Yes, I am still connected to God. God and I have several conversations throughout the day. I am also still connected to God's Word. I just do not attend church every Sunday. My relationship with God has not suffered. If anything, it has become stronger. We church people sometimes look to our pastor as the "be-all and end-all" when we should look to God. My pastor always tells us to read the Bible for ourselves and don't just take his word.

My pastor is a wonderful preacher and teacher. I have been tremendously blessed to sit under his leadership and receive God's Word and God's guidance. I have not entirely left my church; I still occasionally attend services.

For the past two years, I have integrated mediation into my life. Meditation allows me to quiet my mind, quiet my thoughts and center myself. I went to my first mediation class December 2015 and prior to me going to this class, I was having a hard time sleeping at night. I was waking up multiple times a night and waking up tired in the morning. I had a lot of anxiety because I had a lot on my mind. Walking into this mediation class, I was open to the experience. I was open to receive. I met and saw people of different ages from many different backgrounds and nationalities. Everyone was coming together to achieve the same thing, a higher level of peace!

During the mediation class, after several attempts, I was able to finally quiet my mind. That night after my first class, I sleep like a baby the whole night. I had not slept like that in a very long time. This class was amazing and opened me up to a world of peace!

It's a funny thing how God works! He will bring people into your life who are on the same spiritual level. When I started my spiritual awakening journey, I began this journey alone. There were things I was experiencing that I couldn't really tell anyone about because I thought no one would understand, so I spent a lot of time online researching everything I was experiencing. I experienced it alone.

I would have to say that the beginning of 2017 was when God began to bring other people in my life who were having the same experiences I was having. Some of these people were people I already knew. I no longer felt alone. Each person God brought into my life helped me in my awakening on several different levels. No two people God has brought into my life during this stage in my life have served the same purpose. This has been such a blessing for me to find people who are on the same wave length and who are spiritually awake.

Have you ever experienced a time in your life where you felt so full and you couldn't explain what you were feeling? You feel full, light and fluffy all at the same. What is that feeling? It was a wonderful feeling, and I had to know more about it. I did so much research on what I was feeling and then I found it! VIBRATION!

What is meant by vibration? **The Merriam-Webster Dictionary** defines *vibration* as a periodic motion of the particles of an elastic body or medium in alternately opposite directions from the position of equilibrium. In other words, your vibration is your personal energy frequency. It is the energy that surrounds and permeates every cell in your body. In her article, "What is Your Vibration," Sabrina Reber describes vibration as "your divine signature, your soul essence special only to you."

After much research, I found that this "vibration" thing was all the fullness I was feeling on the inside. I was vibrating on a high vibration level and didn't realize it.

Pamela Dussault, in "The Benefits of Being in a Higher Vibration" writes, "The higher the frequency of your energy or your vibration level, the lighter you feel in your physic, emotional and mental body. Vibrating on a high level only means that you experience greater personal power, clarity, peace, love and joy. Your energy is literally full of light. My life flows on a regular with synchronicities."

There is a difference in people who vibrate at a high vibration and people who vibrate at a low vibration. People who have a low vibration sometimes suffer from the inability to sleep. They are to prone to clutter, have attachment issues, and strained relationships. I have suffered from all three of these symptoms at different times in my life. Now, I can recognize when I have low vibration and high vibration. I see things a lot clearer now! I have 20/20 vision!

28

ONE MORE LIGHT

Linkin Park)

Thoughts Transformed into Things

Timelines and time-tables have no place when one evolves on a higher spiritual level! I continue to learn so much and experience so much during this spiritual awakening journey. Not only have my relationships changed, but how I view my energy has changed!

I started taking notice of my energy and the type of energy I give off in late 2016. This was something very new to me because energy to me was what we discussed in Science Class: *Energy + Matter= molecule.* That was what I knew energy to be. Little did I know energy is so much more. Energy is what we as people give off when we walk into a room. Energy is that adrenaline rush I feel on the day of my client's event. Energy is that adrenaline rush I feel right before I get up to speak to a crowd of people. There is good energy and there is bad energy, but I didn't pay too much attention to how each affected my everyday life, Of course, you know by now that "GOOGLE" has become my friend! Off I went to the internet and began researching more about people and energy. I soon began to take note of my own personal energy and what kind of energy I exuded. To me, energy was everything from how I felt in the morning, to how I felt on the way to work, and to how I felt when I got to work. I also began to channel my energy, and I worked to change my feelings about energy in different situations.

When I operate at a high vibration level which is also a high energy level, I notice I feel full, happy and free! It's the most wonderful feeling! Everyone's opinions roll off my back, and I am filled with a love that is unexplainable. I've never known a feeling like this. Yes, I have experienced love in my life. I have loved family and friends and been loved in return. However, I have never experienced love like I experience when I am vibrating on a high level. My frame of mind is different. My mind is refreshed and renewed. I look at life differently. When my vibration level is high, I become deeply concerned when I see someone suffering. I wonder what has happened in their lives to bring them to this point. What can they do to change the course of their life? I am filled with so much more compassion for others when my vibration level is at its highest level. It is such an amazing feeling.

On this spiritual awakening journey, I have discovered something new and incredible. It is the Law of Attraction which is defined as the belief that positive thoughts are magnets for positive life experiences and negative thoughts are magnets for negative life experiences. In other words, you attract what you think.

I tell myself to think only positive thoughts. All my life I had no idea that everything I now have all started with a thought. As a little girl, I wanted to have a woman's presence in my life and I prayed for it to happen. I had no idea all my prayers were being heard. I ended up with not one woman's presence, but the presence of several women. All along, my prayers were being heard by God.

You are what you think you are. Like attracts like. The Law of Attraction is believing a thing before you see it. It is the process of manifestation and is what I consider to be equivalent to one of my favorite scriptures, Matthew 7:7 (NIV): "Ask and it will be given to you; seek and you will find; knock and the door will be opened to you." I have repeated this scripture a thousand times. Ask for what you want, believe you already have what you want, receive it, and be grateful your request was granted! It's all a FAITH WALK.

In May 2017, when I started practicing the Law of Attraction, never in a million years would I have thought I would be practicing this Law or even going into this direction. It started with me feeling there had to be something more than what I had already experienced in life. When I began this practice, I noticed that the things I asked for were starting to manifest themselves. I quickly learned that thoughts become things, whether negative or positive. I work hard to control my thoughts. I only want positive thoughts. Nothing negative!

Sometimes, we don't realize everything we have started with a thought. The house we have, the car we drive, our career, and even our families all began with a thought. It was something we or someone wanted or desired. One thing about the Law of Attraction is that you have to say the things you want and believe you already have them. Then, wait for the manifestation of those things.

Sometimes, we complain because we want a better life, a better career, a better job, or better car. What are we doing to prepare for the better? As we pray and seek God for something, we must prepare to receive that thing. What I also learned is to be specific when I pray. There should be no confusion on our part as to what we are seeking. When using the Law of Attraction, I try to stay true to my original request from God. No matter how impossible my request might be to me, I know it's not impossible for God. This is when my faith comes into play; I must trust God! Finally, beware of thoughts which create doubt in your mind because with God, all things are possible if we believe!

Learn What Sways Your Energy

Anytime I feel joyful, I must be aware of distractions which might sway my energy in a negative direction. Distractions are everywhere, and the smallest thing can change the course of your energy These distractions include people and their attitudes. BEWARE of energy pullers!

This energy thing is serious! A very popular phrase is "Work in Silence". Have you ever been so excited about a dream or a goal God put on your heart? The excitement was so much you couldn't keep it to yourself; you had to tell someone! When you told your plan, all you heard was "That is too big!" or "Are you sure you can accomplish that?" You might even have heard, "I don't know, maybe you should wait." Then, suddenly, the joy and excitement you originally had simply disappeared. All you had left was doubt and fear. In a matter of minutes, your energy level dropped from a very high level to a very low level. This happened because you allowed someone else's energy to sway your energy. This happened to me several times. Now, I don't share my dreams with everybody. The phrase "work in silence" applies here because everyone is not rooting for you. Sometimes, due to their own limitations, people can't honestly see how this thing can be done. On the other hand, I've come to understand that when people are involved in their own world, they might not have the time to be excited about what is happening in my world. I am responsible for staying excited about my God-given dreams regardless of what others say. God gave me the dream, and that's all that matters.

Sometimes, we must put up energy blockers. An energy blocker is something one uses to block unwanted, uninvited and tainted energy. It can be very hard to do because sometimes, you are caught off-guard. You don't see the problem coming. Suddenly, your energy decreases, and you have no idea what happened.

There are times when people see something of value in you and the green-eyed monster appears! They are jealous! They will try to steal your joy. Of course, jealousy is a tool of Satan who comes to steal, kill and destroy (John 10:10). When I think of energy-stealers, I think of the advice given by pop-singer, Kelly Clarkson, in her song, "Catch My Breath." She says,

"No one can hold me back,

I ain't got time for that.

Catch my breath,

Won't let them get me down,

It's all so so simple now."

Overtime, I have learned certain things about my energy and the patterns of my energy. I foresee situations that will sway my energy, and I look to fix the situation before it becomes a problem. Know your energy patterns. Learn the things and situations that are prone to steal your energy and develop practices to protect yourself.

Energy is everything: a smile, a frown, tears, joy, excitement, and sadness. Because energy is everything, it is important to protect your energy from energy pullers.

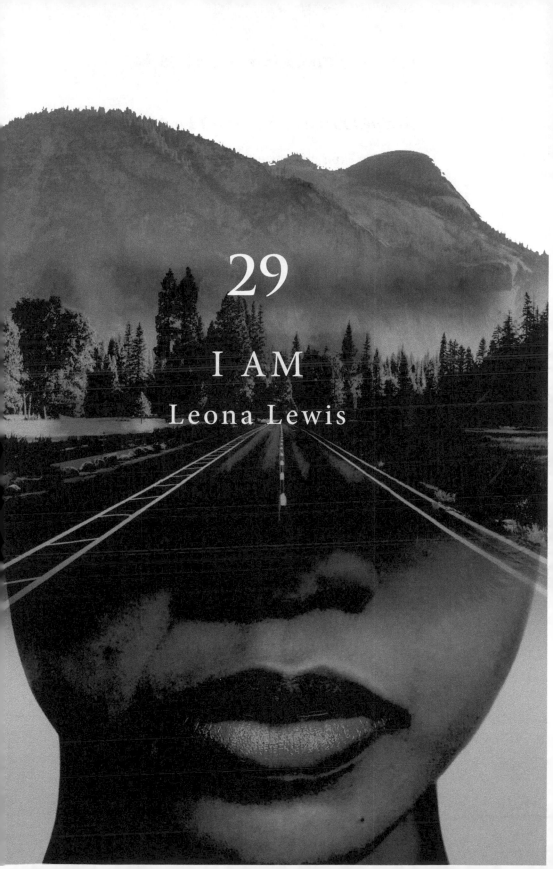

29

I AM

Leona Lewis

Strained Relationships Don't Fit Anymore

There is an expiration date on some relationships. Whether it is a business relationship or a personal friendship, if that arrangement no longer serves you, it will soon begin to distract you from what your goals and purpose are in this life. Life is too short to waste time. We are here for a season and a purpose. There is no time for playing games with people who are not meant to go to the next level with you. When relationships expire, let them go!

Not everyone is supposed to continue with you into the next phase of your life. There were times in my life when I felt I needed certain relationships. When I moved to another stage in my life, I no longer needed those relationships. If the truth be told, some of those relationships drained my energy from the beginning.

I remember one relationship which was fun at first. It came at a time in my life when I was new to the area and had a desire to meet new people and form friendships. I became a lunch buddy with nine of my co-workers, and we socialized after work. I was enjoying this new life when I learned one of the buddies had an issue with me. I couldn't fathom the fact that someone could dislike me! What had I done? I thought I was nice, caring, and friendly.

This friend, whom I considered a close friend stopped talking to me. What was wrong? Some of our mutual friends couldn't' understand why I cared so much. One of them said, "You already know how this person can be. Don't worry about it." I was worried because I couldn't understand why this friend didn't come to me and tell me something was wrong. Then, our friendship got back on track and we were friends again. Eventually, after a few more years of some inconsistencies, a house guest adventure and another fall-out, I was finished with the relationship. It was time to let go! Stephanie had had enough! I didn't need the drama in my life!

This same thing would repeatedly happen throughout the course of my life. The more I evolved as a person, the more my relationships changed. When a relationship reached its expiration date, I willingly let it go. Otherwise, the relationships became strained relationships. Letting go had a cleansing effect on me.

When more of who you are as a person is revealed, it's hard for you to hold onto the wrong relationships and friendships. Holding on is not healthy because it blocks a tremendous amount of your energy. To move forward with your dreams and goals, you must be free of people who are not genuine.

As I continued this spiritual awakening journey, I began to see that other relationships I once valued became more strained. My need to be in certain crowds or groups with certain people changed. I began to gravitate towards people who supported me and wanted to see me succeed and I wanted to see them do likewise. I wanted authentic friendships. What I noticed about this process was that people who were not for me, eventually went on their way. Seemingly, the process automatically happened, and I ended up with the right people in my life. I always keep in mind that God will always bring you who you need at the time you need them. By the way, if someone walks out of your life, let them go.

This is also the same for that job which used to fit and don't fit anymore; and that self-help group you used to go to that doesn't work for you anymore. To live your best life, lose what doesn't fit you anymore. Like a gardener pruning a rose brush to encourage its growth, you must prune parts of your life: trim and totally cut away that which is unnecessary.

No Exceptions to the Game

What I have learned through this process of change is that sometimes, we get in the way of our own progress. We try to make our junk *(feelings and behaviors we haven't dealt with)* someone else's junk, when in fact, our mess is our mess. We can't move forward as functional adults until we deal with our mess.

I look back at the times when I felt I didn't fit in with my own family because I created mental barriers which separated me from them. Another form of **STRAINED RELATIONSHIPS** but this was something I created!

Because my mother and sisters were not around, I always felt a little different and disconnected from my family. I knew I was a part of the family, but I felt apart from the family. This was no fault of my family because they always treated me the same as they treated everyone else in the family. I created this separation.

When my life began to change for the better, my family would tell me that I no longer told them what was happening in my life. How was I to explain that I had found my lane in life and I stayed in it? I wanted to tell them I had begun developing a life of my own by taking what I have been taught and utilizing it in my own way. It was not my desire for them to know every single detail about my life. Whenever I was asked a question, I tried to give my family a peek into my life. I never totally satisfied their curiosity.

This separation was something I didn't mean to happen; it just happened. I honestly can say I wasn't clear on the issues I was having because I hadn't yet gotten to the root of the issue. You can't deal with a thing, until you get to the root of that thing! Once you get to the root, you can move forward with working out the issue. I had to question myself: Why was I feeling this way? From where do these feelings stem? How can I work on the issue? Once I got to the root of my issue, I was able to work on the problem!

My therapist recently asked me, "Stephanie, what is it about you, that when something is said, you get offended?" I had to think! Why do I get offended? Is it because I think someone is always trying to disrespect or belittle me? Why do I think this? Perhaps, I need to conclude that not everyone is trying to make me feel bad.

Being easily offended was a huge issue for me for a long time. Sometimes, I would say, "Everything or person who puts me in a negative mood must go!" This was my way of not dealing with the issue; I was trying to run away from it. Then, I realized this was not always the right choice to make. Running didn't resolve the issue; it only prolonged it.

I knew I needed to work through the issues I was having. I also had to learn what not to let into my spirit because I was internalizing things which should not have been internalized! I tried to convince myself to let pesky issues roll off me, but that wasn't easy. Finally, to make peace with myself, I knew I had to let people be who they are, and I had to be myself. This decision was a huge nugget for me! Golden! I can't control people and what they do or say. I am only in control of what I do and say!

Everyone is on their own journey and there is no time limit as to when a person gets to a certain stage in their life. Everything happens when it's supposed to happen! The time-table I set for my life has worked as far as my career is concerned. I cannot control other areas of my life such as self-growth and family issues because they are not controlled by my own timeline. This is alright; I have learned to embrace this stage of my life. I will be patient and see where the path leads.

I Won't Apologize

Embrace the change and how you feel! Change is hard, and I will be the first to tell you that I do not like change. I love a song Selena Gomez sings about change. In the hit song, "I Won't Apologize," she says,

> "I'm sorry for my changing,
>
> I'm sorry it had to be this way.
>
> Believe me, it's easier just to pretend,
>
> but I won't apologize for who I am."

Yes, change is hard! However, I must embrace the change and I make no apologies. I must embrace my true self because pretending is too destructive.

The song says "Change is Hard". I know this all too well. When I was in the third or fourth grade, our class had a student teacher. She was the best and all of us fell in love with her. Clearly, we didn't know that one day, our student teacher would have to leave us. Well, the time came and prior to her leaving on her last day, I wasn't happy at all. I took it hard. I was heart-broken, and I cried. It was hard for me to deal with the change of her no longer being in our class. You would have thought I would have been used to change considering all the losses in my life, but I was a child and I was not used to people leaving. From that day forward, I knew there would be more situations in life such as this one and I would have to learn how to adjust to change and people leaving! This was a wake-up call for me.

I guess I had no choice but to adjust to change. I moved around so much as a child, it became second nature to me and any resistance would have made it impossible for me to go with the flow.

In 2012, I experienced yet another loss. When I was unemployed, I purchased a beta fish. I named him Jordan. He was red and small, but cute. I loved this fish. Every one or two weeks, I would change the water in his bowl. I fed him every day, and he became like my child. When I went out of town, I made arrangements for my fish to be fed while I was gone. I was so concerned about my fish when I was away. Was he okay? Was he cold? I researched the behaviors I could expect from Jordan. If he puffed up his jaws when you get close to his bowl, I knew he was being territorial. When his color changed, I knew he was not feeling well. I even had a contact at the local PetSmart, and he and exchanged beta fish stories. He was the person I called when my fish was looking blue! I had Jordan for two years. He died on Valentine's Day 2014, and I cried like a baby! I had kept Jordan alive for two years, even after I dropped him on the floor, on the stove, and in the sink. Through all of that, he lived! Then, one day, he floated to the bottom of his bowl and didn't move for a day. I knew something was wrong. After Jordan's death, like any other pet lover, I went to a nice area near a pond where I lived and buried him.

When I had purchased Jordan two years earlier, I was lonely. Having Jordan helped me to focus my mind on something other than my misery. He brought joy to me during a rough path in my adult life. Once again, I had to adjust to change. If you have ever lost the joy of a pet, you know the change wasn't easy.

So many changes in my life! After the 1987 accident, because of my injuries, I had to physically adjust. Then, with all the moving I did as a child, I went from living in peace to living in chaos. I went from living with rules to living with stricter rules. As a scared, lost child, I had to adjust to the way other people ran their household. I believe I mentally blocked out my feelings of wanting a normal childhood and family life, and I just went through the motions of life. I had to adjust to the environment in which I was placed. It was called survival. As I got older and had a stable environment, change became easier to embrace.

Throughout the years, I've also learned to cherish my time with my family and my friends. I've learned to live in the moment because great moments don't last always. It's important to treasure and enjoy every ounce of your time.

Anyone who knows me, knows I love, love, love taking pictures! I love capturing the moments of fun, laughter, and happiness. A picture truly is worth a thousand words. I take photos of everything: food, drinks, scenery, and people. You name it and if it is a part of an event or a celebration, I am taking a photo! Tomorrow is not promised to us, so I think it is important to take as many pictures as you can.

I believe we should say, "I Love You" as often as we can and "I am Sorry" as many times as we need to say it. I also think it is important to address disagreements when they arise. I believe in the saying, "Don't put off what you can do today for tomorrow because tomorrow may never come".

The death of a loved one is the hardest change to embrace. I believe that *no one* can ever get used to death. When my mother and my oldest sister died, felt as if I were in a dream. Had this really happened to my family and me? Was I a motherless child? Did I really lose my oldest sister? Then, before I fully processed the death of my mother and my sister, my baby sister died. I felt even more alone and lost. I felt isolated and yet, there was nothing I could do. Many times, I asked myself, "What am I going to do without Brittany?"

A Hard Pill to Swallow

Just when I thought life was good and couldn't get much better, my family experienced another death! On July 29, 2014, Reece, one of my cousins died. He was more like a brother to me than a cousin. Our family lost a son, a nephew, a father, a brother, a friend, and a supporter. This loss was horrible! It hurt so much, and it was so unexpected! Why him? I admit I was very upset with God about Reece's death, but I later apologized to God and asked for forgiveness.

Reece entered the hospital for an out-patient surgery and never left the hospital. While on the operating table, he died of a brain aneurism. I remember it like it was yesterday. Everyone rushed to the hospital when we got the news because we had no idea what happened. I rushed from work at about 2 PM and headed to the hospital, in Baltimore, MD. When I arrived, my cousin had already taken his last breath! My God! This couldn't be real! Not Reece!

Memories flooded my mind of family reunions, family weddings, Christmas and Thanksgiving travel trips to Chicago, Thanksgiving dinners at his house, weekends when he would stop by our aunt's house and watch television, sleep and wake up singing. The laughs! The jokes! Reece knew all the family history. He was the one who knew how to bring the family together. He was the cousin who gave me money when I got good grades in school, and he was the cousin who on Christmas day, brought me CD's. There goes that love of music once again. Just like my dad and I share a love of music, my cousin and I shared it as well!

Reece was extremely smart. He was a lawyer, real estate guru, an Omega Psi Phi Man, and the holder of two Masters' degrees. My cousin helped so many people in his life.

On the day of his funeral, it was evident Reece had blessed many people's lives while here on earth. Even though his funeral was held on a weekday, the church was packed with people who had come from near and far to bid farewell to a young man who left a legacy of love. I believe Reece was smiling from heaven that day.

My cousin's death was a very hard pill to swallow. I didn't think there was any coming back from this loss. I had a hard time processing this death, and I was angry for a while. No one was expecting this to happen. Reece's mother and my entire family were devastated. Reece was one of my dad's favorite nephews, and my Reece always referred to my dad as his hero. Naturally, my dad was crushed by this sudden death.

I really admired my cousin, Reece. He was the cousin you couldn't wait to be old enough to accompany to the places where the adults socialized. He knew everybody, and everybody knew him. He loved people, and people loved him.

Reece's death was sudden, but I guess in his own way, he was preparing us for his departure. When I heard about some the conversations Reece had with his brother, Monty, and with some of his cousins and other family members prior to his death, it made me wonder if he knew it was time to leave this earth. Do people know their death is near? My only regret is not having told my cousin how much I admired and loved him. I was grateful for everything he had done for me. I wish there had been more time for me to express my gratitude to him for the role he played in my life. My cousin Reece will forever be missed. Three years later, his death still stings.

Embrace Your Pain

Pain is something I have embraced. These memories I have of Reece are memories I embrace to my highest being. I am blessed to have spent such great time with a wonderful human being. At my cousin's funeral, I felt proud to be his cousin. I have often been told that my cousin Reece looked at Megan and me as not only his cousins, but also his sisters. That makes me feel good.

I think the best thing one can do in their life is embrace their feelings. The worst thing you can do is hide how you feel, thinking that if you don't deal with your feelings, they will go away. Embrace them! Feel every ounce of what you need to feel. Embrace the pain, the sorrow, the tears, the fears, the hurt, the happiness, the joy and whatever else you may be feeling.

Embrace your feelings and keep moving. Take the time to acknowledge how you feel, no matter how long it takes. You owe it to yourself to be in that place. If you need to go back and feel it again, do that! Whatever you do, don't run from your feelings.

When you allow yourself the time to deal with your feelings, you allow yourself the time to heal, adjust and change things. Life has a way of bringing things up in your life again and again, and the only way to move on is go through it to get to the other side. Running only prolongs the process. Deal with the issues and feelings at hand. Once you do that, you can move on to what's next.

30

WE ARE FAMILY

Sister Sledge

The Love of a Family I Forgot I Had

Family has many definitions. It can be described as a basic unit in society, traditionally consisting of two parents and children. A family can be defined as a group of persons of common ancestry. I define family as people who are directly related by blood and people who are unrelated but share many common interests.

One thing this life has taught me is that God always give you what you need and who you need. I had no idea who would help Brittany and me after our mother and our sister died. My father was pre-occupied with the loss of his wife and child. He wasn't ready to raise two daughters, but he tried anyway.

Sometimes men have a hard time admitting they need help. I'm sure this was the case with my dad. Thank God for my aunties, my cousins, my grandparents and other wonderful people who lent a hand. God had it all worked out; He knew ahead of time that He would have other family members step in to help two little girls and their father on this journey. Although they were in our lives for a brief time, Grandma and Pop-pop gave my sister and me all the love, guidance, and care that one could ever imagine.

In many different stages of my life, my aunts were always present. I am truly blessed to have such amazing, praying women in my life. My uncles were present as well; however, my aunts had a stronger presence in my life.

Then, there was the aunt who was like the older sister! God was not playing when he said that I would be alright, and he would give me what I needed. Auntie Kim was my mother's youngest sister.

There were fifteen years between my mother and Aunt Kim and seven years between Aunt Kim and me. Aunt K was more like an older sister than my aunt. Throughout my life, this lady has been a wonderful support to me, being there to always talk to me when I needed someone. We have shared many laughs as well. When I was a little girl, I used to follow my aunt around my grandma's house. I know I was probably annoying to her, nevertheless she put up with me. I hope that as she has poured into my life, I have poured into her life as well.

It is said that cousins are your first friends! I believe this statement to be true. I was blessed to grow up with several cousins who were about the same age as me. I had a lot of female cousins and only a few male cousins. We had fun most of the time, but there were times when the estrogen would be too much, and we would fuss and argue. At the end of the day, we were buddies again. Having so many girl cousins helped me feel a part of a family when I was growing up. I always had someone whom I could discuss boys, clothes, music, and anything else with. Having such a large family helped me balance my loneliness when I missed my mother and sisters.

Friends Who Became Family

One day at a summer camp, when I was in my first year of middle school, I met Mrs. Paula. She graciously took me into her life as if I was one of her children. God had blessed me with another guardian angel.

Mrs. Paula, who knew my father's family, became my mentor. She came into my life at a time when I was trying to figure out my life. I had entered the adolescent stage, and this was a difficult time for me. I was young, fragile, lost at times, and not sure of the direction of my life. Mrs. Paula spent a lot of time with me. She'd take me shopping and ask me questions about my future. She really poured into my life in such a way that she was not only my mentor, but she became my family and another Godmother. This lady was beyond sweet, helpful, and caring. She would give you the clothes off her back. Today, I stay in touch with Mrs. Paula and her family. Truly, I am grateful for her continuous presence in my life. I dearly love her.

When I was 8-years-old, I had a teacher, Mrs. Carol Miller, who became one of my favorite teachers. This lady was an angel, and I remember wanting to be in her home-room class. Mrs. Miller and I are in contact today, and I consider her and her husband as family. Recently, I visited my favorite teacher and she prepared a lunch fit for a queen! I was in awe of the love and care she put into this meal for me. The beautiful meal was ready for me when I arrived.

In a recent conversation, I had with Mrs. Miller she proceeded to ask me about my dating life. How was it going? Who was I dating? How Long? What did I want in a relationship? Now, this was not an unusual conversation topic for us because we talked about everything. At the end of this conversation, Mrs. Miller said to me, "Whoever he is, he has to know he is getting a gem. He has to deserve you."

What she said to me that day stayed in my mind because sometimes, when we as women want someone in our lives, we will settle for second best instead of waiting for the best. We will settle for someone who is "half-way there" instead of "all the way there." We will settle for "Mr. Right Now" instead of "Mr. Right All the Time."

I knew I had worked too hard to accomplish so much in my life, to settle for the wrong man. Settling was something I did not plan to do. That day after my conversation with Mrs. Miller, I was even more in awe of my favorite teacher. I left her house feeling like I was floating on air and feeling even more inspired about my life and my future.

Looking at my childhood and my teenage years, I can count on one hand the number of friends I had. Frequent moves hindered my ability to form lasting friendships. Although I am a very caring person who loves and enjoys meeting new people and creating new experiences, when I became an adult and moved to a new area, I thought I probably wouldn't have any more friends than I had when I was much younger. New friendships were not something for which I searched, but I did want to find my own social circle and that I did!

I have been blessed to develop friendships and relationships with people from college, ladies from my church, co-workers from my previous job, the "Golden-Girls," people whom I've met through networking, and both women and men I met while working at my first real Corporate America job more than ten years ago. All these people have greatly enhanced my life. These women and men, I call my friends are family as well. I have a good support group of brothers from another mother and sisters from another mister. Not bad for a little girl who didn't grow up with many friends! These folks really keep me on my toes, acting as a mirror for me and providing tough love when I need it. I am beyond grateful for the people God has placed in my life. Friendship, I believe, is essential for the soul. It's important for you to pour into those relationships, if you expect them to last.

31

YOU'RE MY LATEST GREATEST INSPIRATION

Teddy Pendergrass

Inspiration Which Reaches So Far Beyond

Though it is a love ballad, "You're My Latest Greatest Inspiration" by the late Teddy Pendergrass, reminds me of the people whose influence has molded and shaped a part of my life. Some of these people I've met and know personally. Then, some of them, I have never met. However, through television and through books, I know their stories. Because we do not walk this journey alone, I want to acknowledge some people whose lives inspired me to walk a little taller.

When I think about these inspirational people, I think about Aunt Gloria who inspires me to help, give to others, and show love where there is no love to people who need it. "Family is family and you must help family," she would say. I call this lady the matriarch of my father's family. This retired RN will give you a meal, a place to sleep and a ride to the next town, if you need it. She is always willing to help someone in need. She inspires me to be a better person. I often wonder how she continues to do for others, even though some people are not kind to her in return. She simply brushes off their unkindness and moves on with whatever God has assigned her to do. At the end of the day, God continues to bless her and my uncle. In return, they bless others.

Uncle Kenneth inspires me to be still and not be so quick to move. He encourages me to brush off the frustrations of life. His thirty-eight years of service in the military have served him well. The patience he developed is the patience he tries to instill in me. He is the coolest man you'd ever want to meet. His quiet, peaceful nature and kind heart inspires me to not take life so seriously. "Don't get your panties all in a bunch," he would tell me when I would get upset about things that didn't deserve much of my attention. My uncle enjoys time spent with his family, playing games, laughing, joking and making memories. Watching my uncle enjoy life on a simpler level makes me want to do the same thing: stop, spend more time with my family, and make more memories.

Aunt B. inspires me to do the right thing as a Christian. She is my mother's sister, and she has been my spiritual mother throughout my spiritual journey. When I was growing up, Aunt B. always had a poem or a book to share with me. She lived about two and a half hours from where I lived, and I was always excited when she came to town. I could depend on her to say something to inspire me. Aunt B., a retired English teacher and writer, helped me with my assignments when I was in graduate school. When I was starting my business, she helped me develop the forms I needed. Aunt B. is always available when I need to talk, and she was also there on many occasions when a girl needed to cry and did cry! She'd be right there to talk to me while I dried my eyes. She always offered solutions to issues by helping me to look at the issue in a different light. I am beyond blessed to have her in my life.

Growing up, I used to cry myself to sleep at night because life was scary. I was afraid I wouldn't have anyone to look up to; I was afraid I would be left alone and there would be no one to help me when I needed help; I was afraid of everything! I did not know God already had assigned people to inspire me and help me on my life's journey.

Earlier, I talked about my cousin Reece, a man whom I admired for many reasons. Although he is no longer living, the legacy he left behind inspires me to push towards the goals in my life. He showed me that I could do anything. As I reflect upon his life and everything he accomplished, I think of a man who knew he had little time left here on this earth. I don't know what other goals my cousin had or what else he wanted to achieve, but what I do know is he accomplished his major goals before he died. His work here in this world was finished.

My cousin Reece inspires me to work hard and show love to others while I can because the next day is not promised. He touched so many people's lives and his life inspires me to do those things in life which make me and other people happy.

Television Inspirations

Every time I turn on the television, I am inspired by so many different women and men! These people inspire me to live a better life, a freer life, and a life I enjoy. There is nothing like loving what you do. When you love what you do, you feel at peace.

In 2017, I attended a Janet Jackson concert. I was ecstatic to be able to attend such an event and to be in the presence of what I consider to be greatness.

As I watched Janet Jackson on stage, I noticed the LIGHT in her and the joy she possessed while being on stage and doing what she loved!! I said to myself, "That feeling must be amazing!" I enjoy watching people do what they love. There is a certain excitement and glow that one has when they are doing what makes them happy. Janet Jackson has a certain calmness about herself, the type of calmness which shows she is centered. Janet Jackson was INCREDIBLE! Her dance moves, the chemistry she had with her dancers and band members was outstanding. Janet Jackson inspires me to approach life with that same calmness. She inspires me to be free and do what makes me happy. She was truly a JOY to see!!

Another wonder woman in the world of entertainment who has inspired me to reach for every dream and push towards every goal is Oprah Winfrey! She is the first African American talk-show host I have ever seen. Not only is she an African American doing phenomenal things in this world, but she is a woman, who has used her childhood pain as motivation to push forward and make the best life for herself. I love how Oprah Winfrey uses her platform to help others, sow seeds, build schools, build television networks, and get involved in shows and movies, while keeping a level head about everything. I am inspired by this lady to do what I love and help others in the process of reaching my own goals in life.

Another wonderful inspiration to me was the late Aaliyah Haughton who was a trendsetting and iconic, singer, actress, and model. Although she died at a young age, Aaliyah left behind a body of work her fans will forever enjoy. Through her hard work, Aaliyah inspired me to be true to myself, work hard, enjoy what I do, have fun and live each day to your fullest because the next day is not promised to us. Aaliyah's early demise on August 25, 2001 is proof.

Anytime a music artist that has had such a great impact on the music world, passes on, the fans are generally touched and deeply hurt by the loss of that artist. Legendary artists such as Whitney Houston, Michael Jackson, Prince and Selena Quintanilla-Perez are a few music artists that have influenced my life and left this earth too soon!

Another person whose life served as an inspirational for me was Princess Diana, the Princess of Wales. She was a charitable and giving woman to so many, on so many levels. To me, she was someone, who despite her royal status, wanted to stay true to herself. Princess Diana had a heart for people. Her life inspires me to give to people and help others as much as I can. Tragically on August 31, 1997, Princess Diana lost her life in a car accident. The world may never see another Princess Diana, but the legacy she left behind will live on forever and hopefully inspire other to serve.

Finally, I am inspired by our former First Lady, Michelle Obama, an outstanding wife and mother. During her time in the White House, she rose above other people's pettiness, criticisms, and distasteful comments. Our former First Lady did all these things as she stood strong and firmly by her husband. She even started the Let's Move program, which was aimed at reducing childhood obesity. Mrs. Michelle Obama inspires me to keep moving forward with any project or goal I have despite the judgement of others. She inspires me to believe in myself and create my own path in life and to rise above chaos and negativity.

EPILOGUE

MASTERPIECE
(Mona Lisa)
Jazmine Sullivan)

Sisterhood Pledge

I love Me.

I Love All That I am.

I Respect Me.

I Honor Me.

I Pledge to Never Do Anything to Disrespect Me;

I Pledge to Never Do Anything to Dishonor Me.

This Is Kujichagulia,

And This Is My Pledge.

Author: Mrs. Rachel Polk

Founder of Sisterhood, 1995

Love for Myself and Lessons I've Learned

As a teenager, in the Sisterhood Organization, I recited this pledge more than a thousand times. This pledge had strong meaning for me when I was a youth. It has even stronger meaning for me now that I am an adult. *I love me and I love all that I am!* This has not always been the case for me, but today, I can say this with so much pride. I love everything about me. I love my big forehead, my full lips and my button nose! I love the scar on my face, even though at times, it still makes me feel a little self-conscious. I love my body, I love my personality; I love the compassion I have for others; I love my style and how I like to try new hair styles, and new clothes. I like to live a little on the edge. I love the relationships and friendships I have developed. This has all been a process for me. Because I have spent years working on myself, the journey of discovering my authentic self has been a great learning experience.

I think one of the ultimate goals in life for people should be to get to the place where they find out who they are and love the person they've become. I realize that not everyone fully takes the time to discover their true self. Sometimes, we hide behind relationships and material things. My spiritual awakening journey has helped me look at the simple things in life: long walks, quiet time spent at home, vacations spent with good company, great conversations with good people, and a refreshing workout at the gym. These are all things I value.

I am in the best place in my life. I work to show agape love to everyone I meet; this is the highest form of love.

I find no need to be at war with people because everyone is fighting their own individual battles in life.

This self-love I have for myself is the best feeling in the world. I now respect my own opinion, my own style, my own journey, and my own feelings. Everything I have experienced on this journey has made me who I am today.

What I've learned on this journey is that you cannot run from your problems; you must face them.

To have the type of relationship I now have with my family and my father, I had to do some work on myself. I discovered the walls I put up had nothing to do with my family because they were just being themselves. The walls had everything to do with me and what

I felt. I now feel comfortable enough with my family and others to express myself in a way which gets my point across in a meaningful way. I don't feel the need to run anymore.

Another lesson I have learned on this journey is if there is something you want in this life, you must go after it! If there is a business you want to start, a hobby you want to try, a house you want to purchase, a job you want - go after it! Do it!

When I started my business back in 2006, I had no idea what I was doing. I did a lot of research and I put one foot in front of the other and moved. I would have conversations with myself and I would wonder to myself if this will work, or what will happen if I tried this? Some things didn't work; therefore, I changed direction. I did not quit! All I knew was I had a vision and a passion for doing what I was doing.

My big decisions in life always involve God. Usually, I don't move unless God speaks! When I purchased my home, I waited for God to signal me to move ahead. It took me two years to find my home, but when I found it, it was everything I wanted.

Whenever I am trying to decide whether I should take a particular job, I listen for God's guidance. I am learning to also trust that little tug I feel, my gut instinct. I haven't always trusted my gut feeling and when I have ignored that feeling, I have had a price to pay.

Whatever you do, pray and have faith God will answer your prayers. Prayer is BIG! Faith is BIG! These two components have been major in my life. You can't have one without the other. It's like trying to eat a peanut butter sandwich without the jelly or trying to eat cookies without a big glass of milk to wash down those cookies!

Faith and prayer do hand-hand. Why pray if you don't have faith in your prayers?

Always remember that God hears everything. All the prayers I used to pray when I was a little girl, God heard those prayers. One by one, He answered then.

No tear you have ever cried has been for nothing. God has seen all of them.

Continue to push forward, work hard, stay true to yourself, and know everything will work out for you on this journey we call life.

About the Author

Stephanie C. White is the Managing Director and Lead Coordinator for Stephanie White Events, LLC, an Event Planning firm located in the Washington, DC Metropolitan area. Since the start of her company, in 2006, Stephanie has coordinated several events for her clients and is credited and known for her two signature events, the "Spring Wedding Extravaganza" Bridal Expo & Fashion Show and "A Night To Remember" Fundraiser Gala.

Stephanie currently is affiliated with Premier Bride Magazine, a major publication widely circulated in Maryland, Washington, DC, Northern Virginia & Delaware.

Stephanie's company is listed on WeddingWire.com.

Stephanie has appeared on Washington, DC's WJLA's, **Let's Talk Live** and Washington DC's WUSA9's, **Great Day Washington"**

Stephanie C. White currently holds a position in finance for a local organization. She has a Bachelor of Science degree in Business Administration from the University of Maryland Eastern Shore and a Master of Science in Management with Marketing from the University of Maryland University College. In 2017, Stephanie completed a certificate in event planning from International Association of Professions (IAP) Career College. She is a member of the International Association of Professional Event Planners.

She also holds the position of Special Events Advisor for **Copa Style Magazine.**

Stephanie enjoys reading, traveling, relaxing and attending social events. She currently resides on the Western Shore of Maryland.